Learning German

(badly)

by Tim Luscombe

CLARET PRESS

Copyright © Tim Luscombe
The moral right of the author has been asserted.

www.timluscombe.com

ISBN paperback: 978-1-910461-44-0
ISBN ebook: 978-1-910461-45-7

A CIP catalogue record for this book is available from the British Library.

This paperback or the ebook can be ordered from all bookstores and from Claret Press, as well as eplatforms such as Amazon and ibooks.

Front cover and back cover photos by Marga van den Meydenberg
www.meydenberg.com

Book cover and interior design by Petya Tsankova

Claret Press

www.claretpress.com

For the 48%, and rising

(in lieu of) Acknowledgements

I owe a huge debt of gratitude to friends, family, and all the classmates and teachers with whom I studied German in Germany. They've provided me with the inspiration and ideas for this book. In writing it, I've tried to be true to the spirit of my experience of 2016 – the joy and agony of learning German, the torture of watching a schism develop in England when the UK voted to leave the EU, as well as some life-changing events at home. However, the characters here are cut and pasted inventions. I've plundered lives and experience with no intention of causing hurt or offence, altering and rearranging events to create a book in which nothing is factual and yet everything's true.

Monday 6th June 2016

In Berlin, the seasons announce themselves with more clarity than they do in London. While Sven and I enjoy breakfast on our sunny terrace, fluffy white poplar blossoms dance prettily about in the breeze, marking the evolution of spring into summer, and landing in our jam. But I can't dawdle over cheese and several varieties of cold meat. Having come to the realisation, for about the twelfth time, that I'll never learn German by osmosis, I'm going back to school. I kiss Sven goodbye, and hare off to class.

Excited, anxious and late, I bring my bike to a halt in front of a handsome building that stands uniquely old amongst the modern blocks mostly inhabited by Turkish families on Wassertorstraße. Its neo-gothic edifice of red and yellow bricks is freckled with black metal-framed windows, and, to the pile of bedraggled bicycles chained up in front, I hastily add mine. Pushing open a heavy glass door, I inhale the familiar smell of freshly-cleaned educational institution and race up the stairs clutching my shiny new textbook in search of Room 204.

There's only one unoccupied chair, which I quietly slip into, nodding a silent hello to my neighbours, horribly conscious of the fact that I'm the new boy, though an old boy at that. I seem to be about twice as old as any of them.

Frau Thälmann, our language and integration instructress, is a pale and unquestionably pretty, round-faced woman of around fifty, though I notice she sports a kind of 80s mullet, which is obviously a bit of a worry. To my relief, she's friendly and perky and breezy and jaunty, especially when she insists we don't have to stick to the usual *Sie* formalities. She will *du* me and I can *du* her. "Call me by my first name," she instructs me – in German obviously. We must all speak German all the time. That's the point. It's torture, but we're all in it together. Her first name is Almut.

With the referendum only two-and-a-half weeks away, the

threat of a possible Brexit stiffens my resolve to tread the path to full integration, and thence citizenship. Through a study of language, but also history and politics, it normally takes a year of intensive classes that last three-and-a-half hours a day five mornings a week. Plus exams. Trouble is, I've often had to return to London for work, so I've repeatedly lost my place on the course, and found myself obliged to start afresh with new classmates and a new teacher. I'm joining this group halfway through its journey, at the beginning of the last of the elementary modules, the snappily titled A-2-2. It's taken them a little less than six months to get here, while it's taken me several years.

If I can get German under my belt, I know I can pass the citizenship exam, should I have to. But nothing makes the task easy, because German is tricky. It's horribly tricky. In fact, I find myself mired in a predicament best described by Mark Twain when he wrote that "a gifted person ought to learn English (barring spelling and pronouncing) in thirty hours, French in thirty days, and German in thirty years." Obviously, I don't have thirty years. In thirty years I'll be dead and, even alive, I have little talent.

I've tried French, Spanish, Swedish, Italian and Dutch. I've loved each one but tragically failed to get conversational in any of them. Still, everyone tells me, and deep down I know, that study will allow me a deeper engagement with my newly chosen world. And, having spent half a lifetime in theatre rehearsal rooms telling other people what to do (I write and direct plays), I'm really excited to be on the receiving end of some teaching, and overjoyed to be a student again.

The school's called the VHS (The *Volkshochschule* – literally, the people's high school), and it's hard to ignore the fact that Room 204 is clean and airy and perfectly pleasant. I remember teaching acting in London's equivalent, the City Lit, where every room smelled of gym shoes, however aired it was.

Almut's very much the focus. A square of tables is arranged so that she and her paraphernalia takes up one side (textbooks, pencil case, flask, mascot and an old bread bag a quarter full of sandwiches), while the twenty-or-so of us occupy the other three. To kick things off, she invites everyone to introduce themselves to me by providing their name and saying where they're from. At once, all faces stare in my direction. I'm keen to make a good impression, but I'm so self-conscious that, at first, it's impossible to absorb much. Evidently, I've placed myself between a smiley, pleasant-looking chap called Roberto from Italy and a young, pale woman from China who seems to be drowning in an oversized, blue anorak and is called perhaps Joo? I'm immediately drawn to Roberto's warm, open aura and convivial face, while Joo's evidently a more cautious customer.

Far to my left, there's an Arabic bunch. Fairuz is hefty and dour, and probably the next oldest to me, and Leyla is small and pretty and sports a black headscarf. It's apparent that, like me, Leyla's also new, because next to her sits a young man who's not on the course – her husband. All grim and anxious, he refuses to leave. He's brushed over by Almut, and we don't get introduced.

In the middle, between me and the Arabs, there's an effusion of dark curly hair belonging to several nice-looking girls, most of whom seem to be called Maria. There's some Italians and one other Brit, whose name is Carola I think. She's sort of black, and wears tangerine, or, more charitably, tan-coloured contact lenses. I notice heavily tortured hair and a sprinkling of dandruff. And closest to our teacher sits a young blond man exuding an aura of – well – madness, really. His body unusually erect, he appears to have an oversized head, along with pursed, rosy lips. His skin shines bright. He's not unpretty, in a chubby, Aryan way, and his voice is bassy and bland. It's loud like thunder, but colourless, as if he's speaking from the back of his neck. I think he's from Iceland, and, though not particularly overweight, he gives the impression of having extremely heavy bones. He radiates 'the only gay in the village' and seems totally uninterested in saying hello to me.

My initial sense is that the class functions well. The

atmosphere's friendly, and I'm at once envious of the camaraderie. Because they're so young (Fairuz aside), I guess most of them are launching themselves into a foreign land for the first time in their lives, while I'm already on my fourth migration at least. I've lived – sometimes for work, sometimes for love – in a bunch of European capitals, never settling anywhere for longer than a year-and-a-half. But I've lived in Berlin for more than four years now, which is also how long I've been with Sven.

The VHS's large-sized classes are counterbalanced by ridiculously low fees, which suits me, theatre work paying what it does. Of the many more expensive options, Chinese businessmen and the daughters of Russian oligarchs are generally sent to the Goethe Institute, where it costs about ten times as much, and the teaching has a great reputation. But the VHS is good enough for me, and the German government makes it even cheaper by subsidising EU citizens who elect to study the language. As long as Britain chooses Remain, my ambition is supported by the system.

Once the excitement of my arrival has receded, Almut focuses our attention on the use of *trotzdem* (nevertheless), and I'm teamed up to practise with my immediate neighbours, Roberto and Joo. It's quite shocking that slack-mouthed Joo makes no attempt to pronounce any of the words properly. I mean, God knows what I sound like to a native speaker, but it's clear she's cutting corners when, for *trotzdem*, she comes out with *traz* or *tra*, or occasionally just *tan*. Next, we study the conjunctive. 'I would eat cheese at every meal if it weren't so expensive', for instance. Roberto and I are paired together to work through an exercise which we positively smash, sitting back smugly in triumph and watching the others struggle.

Pretty soon, it emerges that somebody thinks class is all about her. Well, there's always one, isn't there, and this one is called… to be honest, I didn't get her name. In Almut's mouth, it sounds like 'bonbon', but it obviously can't be. She's another hijab-

4

wearing Arab, but she doesn't sit with the others, and is altogether different. She's a talker. When Almut asks her a question, she pedantically describes the level of difficulty of the question, then prissily offers an estimation of the likelihood of her success in answering, before eventually doing so, often cackhandedly. And when she can't bring a word to mind, her MO is to go for loud lingering 'erm' noises. "Eeeeeeeeeeeerm, eeeeeeeeeeeerm." I'm already annoyed by her and it's only day one. The best thing about her is her hijab, which is a wonderfully life-affirming orange.

Tea break announced, I immediately turn to Roberto to strike up a conversation (Italians are my favourite of all the world's peoples), but it takes a while to mentally rehearse a question I feel confident about in German, and by the time I'm ready, he's chatting to someone else. I notice Almut conversing darkly with Leyla's husband, presumably assuring him that no harm will come to his little wifelette here. And then, suddenly, Carola's standing in front of me. Smiling and assured and terribly tall, she addresses me in perfect English, which, after an hour-and-a-half of low-level German is a wonderful relief, and off we go together for coffee. Her relaxed, warm manner makes me feel I've known her forever.

A snazzy handbag hangs from the crook of her arm and she walks with palms up, as if demonstrating that she's the sort of person who's habitually draped with loads of expensive clothes or laden with garlands of flowers. Ploddingly, I inform her I'm from suburban Teddington, to which she replies that she spent most of her youth in Botswana, then modelled in LA and toiled for good wages on Wall Street. The English branch of her family stretches from Reading to Salford, she says.

I tell her about the sleep-reducing ball of anxiety currently squatting rent-free in my stomach, otherwise known as the threat of Brexit, but she doesn't seem too fussed about England's political incubus. I enquire whether she's arranged a postal vote for the referendum, and she assures me that she absolutely intends to. A sister's visiting from LA, you see, so she's been super busy. I hear all about living bi-coastal in the States and how much she prefers New York, and how she's struggling with the grunginess of Berlin, but that sometimes it can be nice, plus there's a lot about America she doesn't miss.

Waiting for class to resume after the interval, I mean the break, I have a go at talking to Chinese Joo. I gather she's here as an *au pair*. She looks so young, I wonder whether she's still a teenager. She speaks a language that, according to her, is "very like Mandarin", and a tiny bit of English with an opaque accent. In German, she reveals she's from *Hochchina* (literally 'High China'), which I'm pretty sure doesn't mean anything, but I imagine mountains. She hasn't the language to reveal more, but seems eager for me to learn, so I draw a map – an oval with two crosses at 2 p.m. for Beijing and 5 p.m. for Shanghai – and offer her my pen. She puts a cross in the middle. Right in the very, very middle.

After class, I should head home and practise German if I'm really to progress. But I have to earn money as well, so my afternoons are ringfenced for work. I was thrilled when a commissioning producer in the UK asked me to devise a new stage adaptation of Jane Austen's *Emma*. The much-loved English novel about class and power couldn't be a more perfect fit for the times. Will pompous, self-sufficient Emma realise her folly in refusing to marry? Will England realise the danger of withdrawing into its own kind of singularity? Everyone knows the book and respects it as a huge cultural landmark, but the Brexiters appear to lack the wisdom that Emma gains when she finally acknowledges her fatal flaws of self-righteous isolationism, turns her back on her own sovereignty, and thus earns the love of Mr Knightley, becoming a fully-rounded member of the larger community.

However, adapting it for theatre is not an easy gig. Austen's narrative is tightly wound up around early nineteenth-century notions of marriage and courtship, and I'm finding it fiendishly tricky to prize my way in. The rules of romantic engagement have been revolutionised since Austen's time, so every situation in which Emma finds herself lacks a precise contemporary equivalent, and I can't see how to tackle it without ripping its heart out, or, to put it less dramatically, losing all the good bits. Additionally, my obsession with the referendum is an on-going obstacle to progress. It's almost impossible to delight in the predicaments of Ms Woodhouse and Harriet Smith, and who-loves-who in empire England, when half the country wants to send us back there.

Despite my obsession, there's not much I can do for the Remain campaign beyond counter Leave nonsense on Facebook. This afternoon, a few friends reach out to the hive-mind with requests for information. Largely musical theatre people who've never read a newspaper in their lives, they know nothing of current affairs unless it's about dancing or cakes, but they feel it's their duty to vote on the 23rd. If they're keen to make an informed choice, I'm keen to send them links.

I notice that a Facebook friend, in a spirit of Europhilia, has shared a time-lapse video of Europe with its ever-shifting boundaries. National colours disappear and coalesce with astonishing speed; century upon century of bloodshed, land grabs, political triumph and catastrophe all collapse into a couple of minutes. It's a sobering snapshot demonstrating the extent to which Europe has been addicted to civil war over the millennia. The graphics don't rest until a few seconds from the very end when, for six decades, affiliation to the European Union creates peace for those inside it. The shapes stop morphing, and the colours remain still. I make a mental note to mention it to Carola tomorrow. She didn't say, but I assume she's pro-Remain, though you never know. Is it too early to friend-request her?

...

The city's most ravishing at the beginning of summer. The shops are full of strawberries trucked in from the dusty, windswept

Learning German (badly)

Brandenburg planes that lie only just above sea level, between here and the Baltic. Asparagus is also at its best – long, white and plump, unlike the short green ones we're used to in England. Germans have a deep-rooted reverence for asparagus and at this time of year they like to talk of little else. Each region has its own speciality, but generally they prefer them served simply and unadorned, with buttered boiled potatoes and maybe a slice of cold ham. They think our thin little green ones are crap.

Only a five-minute bike ride from the *Volkshochschule*, Sven and I live pretty close to the middle of town. Next door is a Russian-owned brothel, and behind that, stands a five-story building for single men, mostly Arabs and Turks. We think it's a kind of half-way house, though we're not sure, and at this time of year, with all the windows open, it's alive with radio stations relaying news from a variety of homes in a variety of languages, much of it a lot more catastrophic than the threat of Brexit, I have to admit. In front of us, across the road, a 1980s ochre-coloured, communist-built block accommodates young Americans who come in the summer to study and party into the night.

Till Sven, I'd never met anyone I would have considered spending the rest of my life with. We're not married, being more like your old-style gays, for whom it's hard to disentangle the institution of wedlock from the patriarchal orthodoxy and Victorian normalcy we campaigned against in the Gay Lib and Aids movements of the '80s and '90s. But after all these years of coming to terms with, justifying and finally celebrating our outsider status, we're now toying with the idea – OMFG – of getting legally hitched. Given the current circumstances, we suppose that it would give us more certainly and security.

There are many reasons why I love him, and I'd like to start with the most superficial: his name. It's very hot-sounding. To be fair, most German male names sound more-than-average sexually charged. Try these out: Florian, Axel, Horst, Dirk, Moritz. I'm not inventing any of this. At the university where he works, those are genuinely the names of his departmental colleagues.

He's very, very sweet and loving, and is one of those people who you feel possesses tremendous integrity. He's much cleverer than I am and, like every good German, terrifically honest, which is great, because I tend to waft through life in a bit of a fantasy bubble, making things up. I've never had much money, but I spend what I've got recklessly. I overdo it with alcohol and food and anything else you can think of. It turns out that Sven's good at curbing my excesses and tethering my delusions. Or perhaps it's just that my love for him is motivation enough to behave a bit more sensibly these days. Gosh, am I making us sound like a pair of old shoes? I just mean he's the 'yin' to my 'yang', the salt to my pepper, and things work out gorgeously well between us.

However, any hope that language learning would be aided by having a German boyfriend was dashed as soon as it became clear that he loves his mother tongue too much to tolerate the effusion of inaccuracies I offer up. Fair enough – baby-short sentences and skimpy vocabulary are enough to try anyone's patience. Also, it would be extremely weird for us to jump into ground-level German when our relationship's rooted in grown-up English, which he speaks brilliantly.

Tonight, we've promised to support a friend of a friend who plays in a band. So after the sun has set, we bike down to Neukölln where he's performing. A mixed area with a high concentration of Turks and Arabs, Neukölln has been internationally famous since Bowie named a track after it on his album, 'Heroes'.

Circling our target, we navigate around a row of seemingly abandoned houses to find ourselves in an extensive but empty courtyard full of jagged concrete and sky. Even though the temperature's still high, it feels chilly. A few brave but desolate blades of grass poke through fissures in rotting stone slabs. It's the kind of place Fassbinder might have got excited about when location-scouting for 'The Marriage of Maria Braun', specifically the scene that takes place during a bombing raid.

Learning German (badly)

At first, my ears are pleasantly assaulted by a burst of ravishing Slavic pop music. Tragically however, it turns out that the Croatian Cultural Centre is hosting a private party and we're not invited. Sven eggs me on past some chained-up bikes, down a curved concrete slope, which leads us even lower into a kind of chilly garage space where the friend of our friend and his three middle-aged band mates plus singer are earnestly applying themselves to bits of old metal sheeting, a candelabra and a bathtub, which, as the evening wears on, slowly fills with water.

Experimental music and noise seems to be all the rage in Berlin, though to me it feels very '70s, or even '60s. Another friend of ours, Adam, regularly secures gigs in bars where he plays obscure cassettes backwards through delay machines, and people flock to listen.

My heart lifts at the sight of a good old fashioned tuba, but the instrument remains unplayed all night long, its only function to be repeatedly thrown into the bathtub, the din it makes varying slightly with the amount of water it meets. The lead singer, a crazy old dame dressed in black plastic bags, screeches and wails and writhes around on the concrete floor, and, as a third act climax, crawls out of the garage and, right next to our bicycles, collapses in a gutter clogged with last year's dead leaves.

We do like normal stuff as well. We're currently very excited about Mashrou Leila, the queer Lebanese indie band, and we'll go almost anywhere to hear almost anything sung by almost anyone who's represented almost anywhere in Eurovision.

Tuesday 7th June

Roberto seems distracted and less friendly than yesterday, which is disappointing because, of all my classmates, I'd identified him as potential new best friend material. Not that I fancy him, but I'm enormously drawn to him. He's so down to earth and good-humoured. And then I realise something's up. He's busy exchanging glances with Almut, who hushes our chattering to inform us that...drum roll...Roberto's found a job. It's a big deal. People applaud. He's tickled pink.

'Poor Roberto', as she calls him, has spent many months traipsing from restaurant to restaurant with his bad German, declaring *Ich bin Roberto* and hoping for the best. At last a restaurateur in Friedrichshain – one of Berlin's party hubs – has taken pity ("*Gott sei Dank*"), and offered him a job as a washer-upper. Almut announces that his monthly income will be a thousand euros, and he smiles proudly.

Crikey but Joo's irritating. She misses whatever point Almut's making by looking up inessential words on Google Translate and texting people in Chinese. Everyone's trying to concentrate on a new grammar point while she delves noisily into her voluminous anorak to produce a plastic pack of brightly coloured sticky labels. Each time she requires one, which is often, she makes a terrible racket carefully unwrapping the pack and fixing one of the labels into her notebook. And the intensity with which she seals it up again is driving me insane. I can't bear rustling plastic. As noises go, it's almost as bad as sniffing.

The vibe in class tells me that, because I chose this seat on day one, I can never have another. I don't want to offend Roberto, but it might be a price worth paying in order to get away from rustly Joo. If I arrive early enough, maybe there'll be room among the Marias.

I want to be optimistic. My brain's all for learning, but my soul doesn't lie. I woke at four this morning from a dream in which I was being thrown into the boot of Nigel Farage's car and deported from Germany. I lay awake for an hour in a terrible sweat, rehashing quandaries about citizenship and health insurance. Then I read online over breakfast about the pound's slide as polls show the extent of British support for withdrawal. In the face of the horror, the single thing that imbues me with any sense of control is applying myself to learning German. But both classmates and teacher are discouraging. They seem to have a very flaky attitude to study. Class is way too relaxed. There are loads of totally new faces today, including orange-ringleted Tracey, who hails from Ireland via Dubai, and a slender Albanian called Bled who buggers off almost as soon as things get going, his excuse being that his flatmate has texted to say he needs to go somewhere. Bled has to return home because they share a bus pass. No one, it seems, is as driven as I am. And punctuality isn't much of a thing either. The big, blond Icelandic man saunters in preposterously late.

He carries a large designer handbag from the crook of his arm, palm up, just like Carola, and slides, without apology or explanation, into his special seat nearest to Almut, separate and aloof. After arranging his bag with the greatest of care on the seat next to him, he wipes his forehead in a gesture that announces he's ready to be taught. It turns out his name is Mervyn. That can't be right, but it's what I hear. He never seems to understand the discussion in class, nor has he yet acknowledged me – a fellow gay man in an otherwise straight-seeming class. I don't think I broadcast my gayness in an obvious way, but why wouldn't his gaydar work? Unless it's simply that he's oblivious to everything that's not him?

Born before decriminalisation, I grew up in the radical seventies, so it's second nature for me to acknowledge another tribe-member out of a sense of solidarity. Mervyn, conversely, must have come out long after many queer battles had already been won, so perhaps it's acceptable for him to be blasé about it.

Or maybe he's noticed and dismissed me as not worth bothering about. I remember when I was his age, a man like me, with a bit of a paunch and a greying beard, would have been invisible. Not that I'm desperate to befriend him, but half a second of eye contact would be nice. I'm overthinking it.

Structurelessly, we discuss *Glück*, which, we're informed, means both luck and happiness. I'm amazed that two English ideas are covered by one German *Glück*. Generally, German seems a very precise language. At least, Sven keeps telling me so.

Since the fall of the Third Reich, Germans have been discouraged from expressions of nationalistic jingoism, and Sven dutifully maintains that he's not proud of the fact that he's German *per se*, but sensibly is quietly happy that it's so. Germany takes care of its citizens with its well-oiled, well-functioning governmental structures, and no one wants for much. However, when it comes to German itself, he's a very proud *Deutscher*, and often impresses upon me how superior to English his language's vast, flexible and robust vocabulary is. In response, I question what kind of value there is in a language in which the simple personal pronoun *sie* can mean so many different things, including 'you', 'she', 'her', 'it', 'they' and 'them'. Being a linguist, he knows perfectly well that English has the greater vocabulary. And I know it, and he knows I know it, and I know he knows I know, but it doesn't stop him coming up with spurious arguments in defence of his mother tongue. And I enjoy letting him boast about it because I love him.

To be fair, while it's occasionally true that one German word means several things in English, it's more common *vice versa*. Take the definite article 'the', for example. Couldn't be a simpler or less malicious word – yet I've so far been exposed to six German words for 'the', and I've a strong suspicion there are more to come. The first cause of this superfluity is that German has a slew of genders. Well, it has three. That's three different 'the's right there. *Der, die* and *das*. Yes, with every noun, you have to actively remember its gender, because you'd be hard pressed to guess it.

Learning German (badly)

The moon is masculine, for example. The person? The person is always feminine, even if the person's a fella! The girl? What else but neutral?! Honestly. It's mad, isn't it? The other day, on the terrace, we were talking about our cactus and Sven commented that "He needed watering." Later, there was a wasp. "Don't move," he assured me, "and she won't sting you." You see? Sweet, but odd. The language, I mean.

As well as having three genders, German's four cases majorly impact on 'the'. They alter everything, disrupt what you've learned and tip you down a rabbit hole of incomprehension. Definite articles and all other parts of the sentence morph in peculiar ways when something stops being the subject and becomes the object instead. Nothing is constant, and it's all very vexing. And you don't have to wait until you reach advanced German to deal with this freakery. No no, they start you off on it immediately. This, as the Germans would say, is 'the toad you have to swallow'.

If this complexity allowed you to express some deeper truths, it would be tolerable, but it's entirely pointless. No linguistic nuance is created by having multiple 'the's. There is nothing to be gained from the fact that the masculine nominative 'the' is the same as the dative feminine 'the', but different from every other 'the'. So I think the whole thing's just a fiendish plot to enrage the foreigner and render German unknowable.

When I complain to Sven about how hard it is, he draws my attention to the glories of the language's celebrated compound nouns, as if they could conceivably compensate for all the heartache. A single German word can have a meaning only renderable by an entire English sentence. My favourite is the word for a dead body that's floating in water – *Wasserleiche* – though one wonders how often it can be used in regular conversation. But that's how I first came across it. Our best friend Bettina wished to tell me in English what part an actor-acquaintance of hers was rehearsing in a TV crime show. He was playing a dead body floating in water.

"What do you call that in English?" she enquired.

"A dead body floating in water," I retorted prosaically.

"My God, sometimes your language is so damned convoluted," she replied in what I thought was a very pot-and-kettle moment.

Some of my favourite compound nouns for which English seems to have omitted to mint a single word include *Erklärungsnot*, which literally means 'explanation emergency' and conveys the distress at not being able to explain your behaviour when you're caught in the act, and *Frühjahrsmüdigkeit*, meaning 'spring tiredness', which is used to conjure a sense of listlessness brought on by the coming of spring. *Kopfkino* ('head cinema') describes the act of playing out an entirely imaginary scenario in your mind and *Kummerspeck* ('sorrow bacon') is the weight you gain due to emotional overeating.

Anyway, back to *Glück* – luck and happiness.

To help us understand its use, we're told a fairy story about a hapless young man – *Hans im Glück*. Returning to his mother after a long apprenticeship in a distant land, clutching his hard-earned gold, Hans is serially hoodwinked by con-artists who persuade him to swap his gold, first for a horse, then the horse for a cow, the cow for a pig, the pig for a goose, and so on, until he ends up with nothing but his happiness. Almut requires us to consider what, according to our own culture, our mothers would do if faced with a child who lost all the gold. "Cry," answers one of the Marias. "Hug me," offers Italian Roberto. "Turn it into a life lesson," chips in Carola. "Seek revenge," proclaims a wild-haired South Korean woman.

Apparently, the way fairy tales conclude in Germany is not with the familiar "and they all lived happily ever after", but with the more pessimistic, "and if those who didn't die haven't died since, they're still alive today."

At mid-morning break, I tag along with Almut and the clique that migrates to a shabby little coffee shop next door. It's dark, musty and unfailingly rammed because all classes break simultaneously. Again, I miss my chance with Roberto when he branches off with the smokers. The trouble is that everyone likes him, but my time will come. Instead, I find myself chatting to a pair of youthful and diminutive Spaniards, both heavily inked and pierced. He sports the word *Liberación* engraved in swirly script above his left eyebrow, and a bright yellow sunflower tattooed all over his bald head. Conversely, she seems to be aiming at a kind of dainty-rockabilly-verging-on-punk look with a magenta bob and Joe '90 specs. Sharing a tatty red cabbage, the first thing they tell me is that they're both vegans. In fact, the way the subject dominates the conversation, they're obviously the evangelical sort, veganism being to the young what Marxism was when I was a youth.

I wrench the conversation away from vegetables in order to describe, in English and probably in inappropriate detail, the car crash that was Sunday night's TV debate between England's warring politicians. But their eyes glaze over. Why am I surprised? It's simply unrealistic to assume that these two are going to know who King-Midas-in-reverse Chris Grayling is.

Attempting to get back on track, I attempt a recreation of the hilarious Patrick Stewart video that's doing the rounds online, in which he plays a prime minister bent on withdrawing the UK from the European Court of Human Rights in a homage to 'What have the Romans ever done for us?' from The Life of Brian. But when I finish, they've not understood at all, and are both convinced that I work for Facebook. It takes me the rest of break to walk it back.

The second half of class is all about agreeing adjectives, and the less said about that the better.

I'm with Emma in Mr Knightley's strawberry beds all afternoon. In the book, it's a gorgeous, funny and troubling scene, but I'm in a dilemma about Mrs Elton's income. Success, I feel, hinges on finding a contemporary equivalent to the grasping, pretentious, hilarious bitch that Mrs Elton is, given that her character is intimately bound up with her money. Trouble is, the difference in financial clout that, for Austen, differentiates Miss Bates from Mrs Elton, and Emma from Harriet, is barely understandable for a modern audience, let alone relevant. I've made several other Austen adaptations and one of the great pleasures of reworking her for the stage has always been that generally no more than a bit of canny cutting and some judicious moving about is required. You end up not so much re-writing as re-typing. But there's something about *Emma* that's got me beat, and, after three hours of brain-churning funk, I'm no further forward, though the kitchen has never looked cleaner.

I bike round to see Jana at teatime for our weekly get-together. She's an old university friend of Sven's, and, as my so-called tandem partner, she uses me to improve her English while I practise my German on her. We've got into the swing of meeting once a week for ninety minutes – splitting time equally between the two languages – during which we gently correct each other's grammar and introduce new vocabulary through conversation. The upside is that I'm less inhibited about speaking one-to-one than I am in a big group, and I don't mind being basic and boring with Jana because she's basic and boring with me. The downside is that, since the referendum campaign has got underway, Brexit's the only topic I really want to discuss and, once launched, I tend to go on about Gove and Johnson in breakneck English way beyond her comprehension, thus rendering the exercise entirely pointless, at least for her.

The husband has commandeered the balcony to manage a hangover, so she pours me a cup of tea and, sitting either side of her kitchen table, we chat in English. Jana's got things on her mind and is anxious to share, describing her job in educational administration. She was initially content, but her duties have gradually become limited to fundraising, so now she's bored. On particularly bad days, she's disgusted with herself for sticking at something so...

Learning German (badly)

I introduce her to the words 'repetitive', 'unrewarding' and 'demeaning'.

She wants a complete break, she says, and dreams of teaching children how to cook, imagining a funky little place in the city where kids could go after school. Given how terrified she is of abandoning her decently-paid job to launch herself on something so uncertain and freelancey, I encourage her to do a bit of research into what she'd need to take the first step.

The phone alarm instructs us to change language. Brushing off her unhappiness, she smiles at me cloudily and, in German, dutifully enquires, "What would you like to talk about?"

Here's a real chance to vent about Gove's performance in the TV debate. Naturally, Jana missed it, and I was only able to catch it because I've downloaded a free VPN, which allows my computer to believe and behave as if it's in England. I'm not sure it's completely legal, but my need to know what's going on back home is acute enough to take the risk. Lacking the emotional restraint to construct proper German sentences, I ask Jana if she'll allow me to express some of what I want to say in English. "Well…" she hesitates, unwilling to break our rules, but I plough on because I believe that sharing my anxiety with others might reduce it. Talking about it has got to help, right?

"When will everyone wake up to the fact," I cry, "that Gove's so-called charm is a ravenous black hole?"

I'm going too fast – Jana can't follow. "Which one is Gove? What is ravenous?"

So I explain that he's "that bumptious squit who describes his pretty hallucination of what Britain will be like post-Brexit as fact."

We briefly get stuck on 'bumptious' and 'squit'.

"Gove's the one who believes, like Goebbels, that if you're going to tell a lie, you should tell a big one and tell it often!"

"Now," Jana encourages me, "you must try to express this in German."

But I know that I won't manage it economically or well. "Just let me say one more thing in English," I implore her, "and then we can talk about something nice in German." Sensing the futility of opposition, she complies.

"How does Gove expect us to trust his facts when the one fact he keeps banging on about," I question her, "is the '£350-million-a-week-to-the-NHS' fact, and we all know that fact's a big fat lie."

"Ah!" Jana has finally sussed which one Gove is. "Yes yes," she shoots back. "He has a... Now what please is the noun in English for a face that must be slapped?"

Of course, the Germans have a word for it: *Backpfeiffengesicht*. Yes, even in Germany, they want to slap Gove's face.

Like most of her fellow countrymen, Jana fails to understand why the Brits are asking themselves whether they should leave the EU, but she's equally puzzled about my fervour. Why, when I talk about it, do I get so frustrated and hot-tempered? Do I have a personal vendetta against this Gove? "Now we must speak only German," she insists, and, reluctantly I agree by telling her, as best I can, about the events of one Saturday evening in March 1966 when I fell in love during the broadcast of the Eurovision Song Contest. Being only five, I was allowed to get no further than the Austrian entry and eventual winner – *Merci, Chérie* by Udo Jürgens – 31 points in the old scoring system – before being sent to bed. But I'd seen enough to convince myself that this thing called Europe was beautiful. Through a black and white telly, it was clear that there was something more colourful in the songs, more passionate in the people and more imaginative in the outfits than anything that existed in my semi-detached-suburban life. Europe, through the mirror of Eurovision, looked a bit like what I knew, but was significantly different. Same but different. And, without having the words for it, I kinda sensed that was me too.

I explain to Jana that the next momentous date was January 1st 1973, when Britain joined the EEC, which in those days was thought to be all about industrial supply chains but, aged twelve,

Learning German (badly)

I knew was really about peace. Racism was a pretty fundamental part of life in the '60s and '70s, as was anti-Semitism and a society-wide terror of anything gay. As a twelve-year-old schoolboy, it was evident that membership of something larger and more diverse than the UK might dilute the difference I felt and facilitate a fight back against the bullies. And when, in 1992, the Maastricht Treaty transformed me into an EU citizen, life truly began. I could live anywhere on the continent I wanted to, and I did.

I explain to Jana that, when they think about Europe, most of my countrymen imagine, at best, the prose of economic gain, while people who share my fetish for all things European invariably hear the poetry of pan-continental brotherhood. Why is it so hard for those with no memory of the 1930s and '40s, I ask her, to engage with the idea that a union of countries is, at the very least, a bunch of people who aren't at war with each other? But historical memory is short. I recently read that one in twenty Brits doesn't even believe the Holocaust took place. Brexit seems set to prove that a community can't sustain the memory of pain longer than three generations. Can it really be the case that every seventy-five years, people need to experience a whole new wave of torment before, they're once more prepared to declare that 'nothing like that will ever happen again'. It's at this point that Jana begins to get my drift, or at least, she looks concerned and stands up to make another pot of tea.

Knowing our session should be coming to a close, Lilly joins us. At eight, she often makes us unobtrusive little visits. She's quiet, not shy, but I've never seen her particularly happy. She's finished her homework, and wants permission to do something else. Leaning into her mother's ear, she's a susurrating squirrel seeking physical contact. Her dad's not in a state to be talked to, and her brother's in his room busy with boy things. I've only met twelve-year-old Lukas once, when he opened the door to me and scampered away as soon as he reasonably could. Jana tells me he's earnestly engaged in ecological matters and spends every evening saving the world online. Both children are super well-mannered. I know they go to an ordinary local school, so all I can imagine is that an ordinary local school in Germany is better at creating pleasant children than an ordinary local school in England.

While Jana deals with Lilly by fixing an apple juice and having a little chat, I begin to wonder about the difference between the two countries in terms of basic manners – the oil in the machinery, in other words. There is a distinction to be made, there's no doubt about it. Perhaps respect and good manners are more highly valued here. Soon after my arrival, I instinctively found myself trying to be more polite in order to seem more German.

For a German, being punctual does not mean arriving on time, but arriving early. And when it comes to the way people address each other, what Brits might think of as superannuated is very much still *de nos jours* here. Even in the most relaxed work situation, whatever one's age, one is addressed as 'Mr' or 'Mrs' until one suggests, or one is invited to be otherwise. Even an invitation to a casual party is composed with something of an eighteenth-century flourish. And, however informal or intimate a gathering, I found to my great embarrassment that you mustn't eat or drink until everyone's taken their seats and the host, or the group's senior representative, has invited you to begin, usually with a toast. On a lavatorial level, I was quite astounded to realise that German men pee sitting down. They're mindful of the next user. They aim to minimise the splash.

I don't believe it's too grand a statement to claim that politeness is a political matter for Germans. While it might be true that the English need to kick over the traces every seventy-five years, the Germans are more aware of a need to retain the memory of the twentieth century. Reflecting on a micro scale the macro concern about their post-war reputation, they're highly sensitive about the impression they make in public places, where they're determined to conduct themselves irreproachably and cause no offence. So, compared to Brits, they tend to speak at the level of a whisper when they're out. I'm always telling Sven to speak up, and he's always telling me to quieten down.

And yet, weirdly, my German pals often inform me, with absolute conviction, that it's the Brits (football fans and stag parties aside) who are the polite ones, and certainly the most formal. They're all convinced we talk to each other like we're in 'Downtown Abbey'.

Formality might play a part, but I'd say it's definitely not politeness they observe when they watch Brits in ordinary conversation. German has no word for the rococo obfuscation of normal English exchange, so they're reduced to calling it politeness when it isn't. In comparison, Germans converse with ruthless clarity. They're encouraged by their language which, notwithstanding tortuous grammar, can be phenomenally, refreshingly direct. In fact, with German you're *required* to be straightforward. If you don't use proper sentences, you won't be understood. So they never 'talk around the hot porridge', as they say.

While the English woman might ask, for example, "Would you mind very much if I also brought my sister with me?", the German translation would be, "Can my sister come?". But not only does the Brit pirouette around a question (making it so vague that she couldn't possibly cause offence or confer obligation), but she also lies her head off with the answer. The response to the question, "Can my sister come?" in German will be "Yes" or "No", "Yes" meaning yes, and "No" meaning no. The answer in English might be, "Oh, your sister? Great! Of course, bring her – the more the merrier", which sounds very much like 'yes' but could easily mean 'no' with an implicit invitation to study further remarks in order to elicit which way the wind actually blows sister-wise.

Germans aren't straightforward by accident. Aside from the demands of their language, their active resistance to anything vague, indirect and hyperbolic is rooted in their obsession with absolute truthfulness, which in turn springs from a religious idea about being true to oneself. Our 'politeness' may fascinate them, but it's not necessarily something they admire. In fact, it's often regarded as suspicious, especially when it's used, as Brits sometimes do, as a cowardly form of hypocrisy. In Germany, bluntness is a virtue and insincerity a crime.

People won't open gifts in front of each other because it's impossible for a German not to voice a truthful reaction. If she hates it, or it's a duplicate, she'll jolly well tell you. On my last birthday, when I received a DVD I already owned, I lied and pretended to be thrilled. Sven couldn't understand. "You must tell the truth," he insisted. "But," I replied, "telling the truth would be hurtful." For Sven – and he's typical – lying would be worse.

In the cause of honesty, if you relay a funny story at a dinner party, be prepared for your loving partner to help you out with factual corrections. His interruptions will not make for an effective joke-telling style. Your timing will go all wonky because you said something happened a week ago when it was actually eight days. You won't get the laugh you were after. But at least you'll have been completely truthful.

In a society that regards insincerity as an injury, small-talk is a bit of an issue. Under communism in the East, it was regarded as the acme of decadence, opposed to working-class hegemony. Even now, more than a quarter of a century after the fall of the wall, it's seen as vulgar at best. Our Sunday brunches often bear the brunt of our East German friends' reluctance to indulge in it.

Because Germans prefer unadorned truth, they're not in the habit of recognising, let alone appreciating, any kind of non-literal linguistic meaning. It's like dealing with Americans. You have to be terribly careful with, say, irony or understatement. Compare the English and German versions of 'Bake-Off', and you will immediately see what I mean. In Germany, it's a show in which people bake cakes – which are then judged. There is no humour, innuendo or charm. Can you imagine? In loftier thought, the philosophical Anglo-Saxon might look at the world around her, acknowledge that it's mad, pointless and cruel, and say something undercutting, withering or ironic. The philosophical German has an equally clear understanding of the situation, but she's more likely to spend the day under the duvet aching with metaphysical pain, i.e. feeling the *Weltschmerz*. It's another top German compound noun that means more than its literal translation – world-ache. It's the despair you feel when you realise the truly purposeless nature of everything.

Perhaps I'm stretching this beyond all bearing, but I see a link between the German tendency to account for things conceptually, and their inclination to reach out for a Big Idea when facing a challenge or a crisis. While a German will search for an elegant and beautiful system – a one-size-fits-all operating philosophy – an Englishman will more likely adopt a prosaic approach, building from the bottom up, all scrappy and piecemeal.

As evidence, look at the history of the twentieth century when the Germans reached for the Big Ideas of, first, fascism and subsequently, communism. Big, yet hardly great, either of them, as it turned out. Nonetheless, these days it's Germany that has perfected the evolution of incremental, uncontroversial development, and Britain that looks eager to throw away forty years of beneficial cooperation for an idea that's as oxymoronic as good communism. The Leavers would have us believe that a glorious future of free-trading relationships is to be achieved by abandoning the world's largest free-trading area. They argue there's sovereignty to be won by turning our backs on an institution that's guaranteed peace, protected workers' rights and safeguarded environmental standards for half a century. Instead, elitist extremists like Liam Fox and Jacob Rees-Mogg wish us to embrace the privatisation of public services, the release of corporations from regulation, and the pursuit of dodgy deals with disreputable countries. If it's a case of wrenching back control, it's certainly not Fox and Mogg I want it returned to.

Wednesday 8ᵗʰ June

There's trouble with the neighbours. A young and we-think-Libyan family has moved into the apartment on the mezzanine floor of our building, and against all the rules, has taken to leaving shoes outside the front door overnight. The culprits – two pairs of adult shoes and two adorable tiny pairs of kids shoes – are scattered about all over the landing exactly where the other inhabitants pass on their way in and out. This arrangement involves a lot of tiptoeing, and, in Sven's case, fulminating darkly.

This morning, as I set off for the gym, I can hear an argument has kicked off. A neighbour from the third floor is instructing the North Africans that the reason they may not leave their shoes out is because it creates a trip hazard. And they may not chuck furniture they don't want into the courtyard either. The trash men do not take furniture away. Look, there's a sign here in the hallway with a number to call for the appropriate agency. And they must keep the main doors shut, front and back, at all times. People have been known to sneak in and camp out in the lock-ups below. But most of all what they may not do, the righteous neighbour insists with an ever-harshening tone, is hold tea-parties for their Arab friends in the cellar. No open flame! No open flame! The neighbour is making himself as clear as dumpling broth, as the Germans would say.

In a way, I'm glad. The Libyans are a bit of a liability with their windows blacked-out with hideous dark brown rugs. There's a stream of dodgy-looking visitors traipsing in and out at all times of the day and night, and the kids never seem to go to school. But what do we know about their situation? And how do we expect them to know the rules when they don't speak German and can't read the house-notices? Either way, I'm not getting involved, so I pretend not to understand the conversation, as I stealthily pick my way through the shoe hill. Like the coward I am, I bid the warring parties a cheery '*Guten Morgen*' and disappear sharpish.

In class, Leyla, the youngest of the Arab women, has shaken off her husband (Bravo, Leyla!), and it's she who proudly instigates a present-giving ceremony, for today is the birthday of one our classmates.

Hiding under her black hijab and long, heavy, dark overcoat which, despite the heat, she never takes off, Leyla's made little impression on me so far. But there's no ignoring her today when, beaming from ear to ear, she proudly bears aloft a handsome homemade cake to lay in front of the Korean woman, whose name, if I hear correctly, is Jang-Mi. Almut sings Leyla's praises. Considering that Ramadan's underway, contributing a cake is positively heroic. And then our teacher makes her own offering: a bunch of small but bright roses in a sweet little vase. The tattooed Spanish girl lugs in an ugly, misshapen thing that looks like it's been constructed from melted Bounty bars (so much for veganism), while Carola and Icelandic Mervyn have joined forces to buy a tea mug and a packet of tea. Fairuz's gift is a clip-lock box, and when Jang-Mi fails to inspect it, she snaps it open and makes her smell the food inside. My neighbour Joo brings nothing, but, after candles have been lit and the small pile of gifts have been assembled into a shrine, she leaps up, runs over to it, rapidly snaps a photo and scurries back to her chair. Jang-Mi is lost for words (at least German words) to thank everyone. But however much she keeps her face covered with her hands, she can't entirely obscure a delighted smile.

As the celebrations intensify, I feel even more the interloper new-boy than I did on day one. I've brought nothing because no one told me it was Jang-Mi's birthday. And when Mervyn dives into a book cupboard and brings out plates and forks for the cake, this sweet little ceremony starts to become truly aggravating. I feel excluded, though no one's excluding me. I hate the tyranny of spontaneous cake joy because I've done enough office jobs to know that the Vacuous Ones use cake to overthrow natural democracy with their loud, jolly tyranny.

Almut attempts to justify the lesson's collapse by teaching us a German birthday song. But I already know the stupid ditty from the last module. I've since discovered that no German actually sings it, because they all prefer to sing 'Happy Birthday' in English. Not to mention the fact that this morning I nearly bust a gut getting up early to make it to the gym before class, arriving in Room 204 punctually and with homework done. Yet here we are chilling, as if time has no consequence and I've made no sacrifice in my writing schedule. I'd be surprised if this sort of thing happens at the Goethe Institute.

Next to Jang-Mi is her husband (also Korean), and he's deputised to dish out the cake. He understands that the Arab ladies can't have any (because Almut's explained Ramadan four times to him), but he's puzzled by my refusals. I've turned down two slices already. Unsure whether I'm just being polite, he's determined to get me to accept some, so he comes round for a third bid with desperation in his eyes. I panic and mumble something in English about not eating sugar, which is a lie, but I sense that, while his English could cope with "I don't eat sugar", it would struggle with "Well, actually, I'm gluten intolerant, you see – no, it's ok, I'm not allergic – no, not celiac – just sensitive". I'm a cake-refusing, curmudgeonly old fart. Why do I resent the group's bonhomie? I admit the truth: I just want to cut short the time before I can feel a legitimate part of it.

With only ten minutes left before the break, the lesson finally begins, and Chinese Joo, who, when she isn't eating cake, spends the morning doodling, is tasked to read aloud a brief passage on the subject of migration. She sees '*ihr*' and says '*ich*', and Almut lets it go – her guiding principle to allow us to speak freely at all costs. Nor does Joo acknowledge punctuation. She takes a breath whenever she needs one, so everything's chopped up and nonsensical. She obviously understands nothing of the passage she's reading.

Learning German (badly)

When Almut pronounces her name, it sometimes sounds like Joo and sometimes like Shoe. Oh dear, what to do? Joo herself rarely speaks if not directly addressed. Left to her own devices, she's either mute or goes off on incomprehensible rambles dense enough to preclude questions, because questions are her enemy. If you ask her something, she'll respond by wildly shouting random words and searching your face for signs of recognition. So, overall, it's hard to make any progress. When not rustling or doodling, she sits, lost inside her navy-blue anorak that's more like industrial cladding than a jacket, and taps away on her phone. It's hard to discern any character in her at all, unless wearing an anorak is a personality trait. The European football championship is fast approaching, which perhaps explains why, from nowhere, she suddenly blurts out "Barcelona". "Barcelona!" she shouts. Then silence. She's quite a mystery.

Who rides bikes?, Almut wants to know. All of us, that's who – with the exception of the girl largely responsible on day one for creating the impression of masses of black curly hair. I think she's Cuban and possibly called Mira and she's horrified by the notion that anyone would think she rides such a modest form of transportation. But the rest of us proudly navigate town on two wheels. It's cheap, fun and the road traffic isn't nearly as rageful as it is in London. The city's pretty level – a couple of hills here and there, but nothing too strenuous. Designated lanes are routinely built into pavements. But they're often only subtly demarcated, so it's easy to terrorise tourists who aren't used to looking out for bicycles haring through pedestrianized areas, especially round Potsdamer Platz where so many of the uninitiated gather.

Even if you mount the pavement illegally, Berliners won't abuse you, believing you've done nothing worse than exercise your rights. Furthermore, cars are obliged to give cyclists a luxurious metre-and-a-half berth, allowing you, Sven contends, to tell which drivers are from old West and which from old East Berlin. Before unification, an *Ossi* driver (East German) wasn't obliged to give any space at all. When East Germany became absorbed into West Germany, the two countries weren't united as equals. The East had to westernise – there was little discussion about it – and West German rules now apply throughout the land. So if you're ever cut up by a car, Sven claims you can be pretty sure it's being driven by an unreconstructed *Ossi*. But then he's a bit prejudiced against them, so he would say that, wouldn't he?

The German traffic light is one of the few exceptions to the rule that everything in East Germany had to westernise when the two states unified. West Germany's waiting and walking traffic light figure was a humdrum human, while the equivalent in the East was specifically male, wore a hat, and was beloved to such an extent that he even survived the *Mauerfall* (the fall of the wall). Today, the *Ampelmännchen* (the little traffic light man) has achieved cult status and is seen way beyond his light, assuming all sorts of shapes and sizes from keyrings to designs for cushions. As a tourist, it's hard not to visit Germany without buying a small green communist and taking him home with you.

In my opinion, there's a pressing need for more *Ampelmännchen* at the many crossroads where nothing on the road informs you who has priority. You learn by experience that it's yours if the other vehicle is coming from your left, but, if it's approaching from your right, you should wait and let it past. Having habitually messed it up when I was first here, and frequently nearly got myself killed, today I'm the one most likely to shout at an ignorant tourist who fails to give me priority when she should, or dithers when she needn't.

And roundabouts? There are hardly any! Yes, there's the iconic communist-built monster containing a giant workers-of-the-world-unite-type fountain on Karl-Marx-Allee, and there's the road around the tourist-must-see Siegessäule, a monument to commemorate some of Prussia's many war victories. But, apart from those, they're extremely rare. Not only that, but, bizarrely, the rules for navigating one don't necessarily apply to any of the others!

Learning German (badly)

...

On Sven's return from work, we head several miles north of the inner-city, up to Weißensee, for our friends Jost and Jochen's first barbecue of the season. It's a hell of a schlepp, but always worth the effort because Jost is a great and generous cook and a maker of wonderful alcoholic concoctions, and their place is really pretty.

It's kind of a dacha – a tiny but fairytale-ish second home that looks like the kind of woodshed Little Red Riding Hood's grandmother might own – and it's set snugly in the centre of a sizeable rambling garden. In normal life, Jost and Jochen base themselves on the Baltic coast and work in tourism, but the dacha is where they seek refuge whenever they visit Berlin. We know the pair from clubbing days. Not that we do much of that anymore.

We park up against a cherry tree at the front, unable to resist picking a few perfectly ripe, swoonily delicious fruit, before setting off through the uncut grass and a mass of strident peonies and irises overflowing their flower-beds. There are sweet peas of every imaginable pastel, and a settlement of over-the-top roses surrounded by an lake of powder-blue cornflowers. There are picturesque little islands of chairs and tables cobbled together from bits of found wood, a smoking barbecue and, separately, a great metal fire-pit-type-thing. This time, there's an additional guest as well.

We're informed that Kamal, a twenty-seven-year-old Syrian with beguiling eyes and a mild manner, has only lived in Germany for six months, during which time he's been adopted by Jost and Jochen to be...well, it's not fully explained exactly what position he holds in the family. Suffice to say, he and Jost seem especially fond of each other. Though shy, he's made himself comfortably at home and has prepared salad and dips for us.

Sven's favourite thing in the world is to make a fire, so he keeps himself busy lugging wood about, arranging it scientifically in the cauldron and forensically prodding the blaze, while Jost tells us, without seeming to boast, that he and Jochen have found housing and employment in their seaside-based business for half a dozen Syrian refugees, including a married couple and their ten children. Our German friends even arranged the kids' extraction from Syria and the transport logistics to get them all the way to Germany.

By contrast, they got to know Kamal under entirely different circumstances. They found him on Scruff, the gay dating site.

I'm eager to quiz him about his journey to Europe, so we sit together and talk. His English is fluent and, as far as I can tell, his German's already better than mine. First, he's keen to establish that he was a soldier in the Syrian army when ISIS emerged. The Islamic State, he explains, believes that the way to deal with a homosexual (soldier or not) is to take him to the top of a tall building and throw him off it. So, when it claimed hegemony, Kamal and two friends, both soldiers and both gay, decided it was time to leave.

He describes the two weeks it took in Izmir to negotiate a boat ride to Greece. The three comrades traipsed from one end of Hungary to the other, permanently hungry and never sure where they'd sleep. When they were finally on the point of entering Germany, they narrowly escaped being rerouted to the Czech Republic against their will. But in a little over six weeks, they made it, and in one piece.

While Kamal sits in front of me – charming, open and urbane – talking about the challenges of learning a new language, hunting for a job and doing what he can for his family back in Syria, I can hear Sven complaining to Jost and Jochen about the suboptimal entertainment facilities we were forced to endure flying Air Berlin to Sri Lanka for a three-week vacation in February.

Kamal asks for neither sympathy nor praise. He rejects the term refugee for himself, and reminds me that the history of Europe is the history of migration. The first European, he informs me, was Europa herself, who, raped by Zeus (manifesting himself as a bull), made the perilous sea journey from Libya to Greece straddling his back and clinging to his horns, thus instigating the story of migration to Europe's shores that continues to this day. Kamal insists he's no more, but no less, than a modern-day Europa.

Jost and Jochen have found a house for him in Jochen's old hometown, and the German pair enjoy taking him around to show him what's what. While we gorge on steaks and koftas, our hosts recount the events of Saturday night. They accompanied Kamal to *Gayhane*, an event for the queer Balkan crowd at SO36, one of Berlin's most legendary clubs. The young man was shocked and delighted to see so many others he knew from the gay scene in Syria – friends he'd said goodbye to in Damascus, having no idea if they'd ever meet again.

The close-to-a-million Syrian asylum seekers who recently arrived in Germany added 1.1% to the population, a figure the government described as 'manageable'. Simultaneously, Prime Minister David Cameron categorized asylum seekers stuck in Calais as a "swarm". By that stage, the UK had only admitted 166 Syrians, a figure so pathetically small that even xenophobe Nigel Farage suggested it could be increased.

From a language-learning point of view, it's amazing to reflect that the influx didn't create a bottleneck at places like the VHS. But the German government simply threw money at teacher training and generated hundreds of new posts. As Labour MP Tony Benn once put it, "The way a government treats refugees... shows you how they would treat the rest of us if they thought they could get away with it."

Thursday 9th June

I open my eyes exhausted after another night punctuated by periods of wakefulness. When I say wakefulness, I mean a kind of fevered semi-consciousness accompanied by a racing heart and images of penury rampaging behind my eyelids like unherdable sheep. The fact that no specific fear identifies itself among this amorphous mass of anxiety is part of the hell of it. I'd like ex PM Cameron to know what he's done to me, but since he decided to risk the future of the country to buy off his party's right wing and reassert his own position, I don't suppose my wrecked sleep is a by-product he'd be particularly concerned about.

When I see an email in my inbox from Dad, I assume it's about some logistical aspect of the plan Sven and I have to visit him and Mum in Teddington in ten days' time. It's a very rare thing to get an email from my father. Mum's the communicator. But it turns out that he doesn't want to talk logistics. He wants to know what my take on Brexit is, because many of his friends and neighbours seem to be hinting that Leave's the way to go, and he wonders if he's missed something. Surely, he argues, the right thing is to Remain. Of course, no one in the street would be crass enough to stick up a campaign poster in their front window, he explains, or get into an actual debate about the subject at the Bowls Club or in the car park in Tesco's, but he just senses that there's a Leave-oriented surge in the county and that, politically, he and Mum feel a bit isolated. Christ, if Middlesex warms to Leave, we're well and truly screwed.

I write straight back to reassure him that he's missed nothing, to stand firm, and that I hope it goes ok at the doctor's this morning. It's just a routine check-up. He takes about a thousand pills for a hundred different things, so he's constantly being poked and prodded and measured for things.

My arrival at school coincides with Mervyn's. His hair is

conspicuously golden, his handbag especially lacy, and I'm determined to find out what his name actually is. To break the ice, I enquire how easy it is, being Icelandic, to live in Germany. I'm genuinely interested in his case because Iceland's outside the EU, which Britain might soon be. I'm more than casually curious about the bureaucratic implications.

"My country is in the EU", he replies.

"Is it?" I'm pretty sure Iceland isn't a member, but it seems rude to insist. So I retreat to safer ground and quiz him about his name, only to discover that I've heard correctly and it *is* in fact Mervyn. His body language suggests he wishes the conversation were over, but I'm undeterred. "Is it common for people to be called Mervyn in Iceland?"

His response is curt. "Who said I'm Icelandic? I'm from Estonia!"

"You're *Estonian*", I'm flummoxed. "Why on earth did I think you were Icelandic?"

"Everyone does", he says, with dramatic resignation, "especially the Anglo-Saxons. You have thick ears. But there is a difference between *Estland* and *Island*. Anyway, you never believe anyone actually *comes from* Estonia. But *I do!*" he brays triumphantly as he stalks into the classroom, greeting our classmates like Grace Kelly might.

Lovely Roberto's away, and his chair – the one to my left – is occupied by the Korean man. Surely the cake incident and all the associated loss of face would have warned him that I'm to be avoided. But no. He's delightfully warm and friendly, and, when I smile at him, he smiles back at me, and asks how I am. "A bit worried," I reply. "About German language?" he asks sympathetically. "No, about Brexit". "What is Blexit?" he enquires.

Fabulous news today is that noun gendering is not entirely random. For example, all trees are feminine. Our instructress provides *die Pappel, die Linde* and *die Eiche* (poplar, linden and oak) and asks for others. "Mimosa," responds tattooed Spanish girl. "Very good," replies Almut. But the woman with the orange hijab, the one who thinks everything's about her, takes this as her cue to deliver a colourless, toneless and agonisingly halting aria about the cultural significance of mimosa – about how it is very common in Tunisia and how, in Italy, it's traditionally given by a man to a woman on International Women's Day.

Turns out, as well as Arabic, French and some German, she speaks Italian too, and relishes every opportunity to demonstrate the fact. She uses Roberto to do this, wasting heaps of time by insisting on translating interesting things into Italian to impress him. Then *he* takes up the mantel, creating a perfect storm of tedium, by lengthily informing the class how all this applies to life back in Palermo.

On the subject of mimosa, for example, I'm perfectly aware of its symbolism and use on International Women's Day, having lived in Rome for a year myself. But, unlike orange hijab woman, I choose not to employ my shockingly poor German to share this knowledge with the class because I believe it would be irrelevant, tedious and just plain showy-offy. Or am I just a dick? Am I, in fact, jealous of her willingness to say stuff out loud despite her skill level? As the Germans would say, you can 'take poison on the fact' that what she says is a lumbering torrent of syntactical fails and grammatical clusterfucks. But accuracy isn't the point. Content isn't the point. The fact that she talks in German – however badly – is the point. I'm not prepared to sound stupid or lame, but *she is*. And the fact that she gives it a go means she improves, and the fact that I won't means I don't. Pride, pride, wretched pride. And dickery.

Self-identifying as a European rather than a Brit, I've written plays about European identity and mounted productions in theatres all over the continent. However, like Sven and his love of German, I admit that my sense of myself is also inexorably tied up with the one thing I definitely don't hate about England – its language. I wish it wasn't so. I wish I could let go, like orange hijab woman does, and embrace a whole new me; a me who confidently expresses himself through ham-fisted German. But I'm trapped in my English Englishness. Without linguistic precision, I feel disorientated, no longer sure what truth is. I need clear words, lucid meaning. I'm Brecht and Thomas Mann in California, except less talented and less successful. My *Heimat* is the language of the country of my birth, not the country itself, and like the Germans in wartime Hollywood, I face the task of having to develop a whole new set of tools in order to be fully me.

It goes way back. At school, as soon as I realised that being rubbish at games was a liability, I constructed a social mask from the power of words to defuse and seduce. I understood that jokes often make friends more effectively than a talent for sport does. And I spoke fast, because I intuitively knew that humour is more about the pace of delivery than the words you deliver. The way I deliver German – slowly – is death to comedy. And yet I'm expected to remove my mask in front of people I don't know in order to reveal a naked quaking idiot who can't decide which definite article to use? It's too big an ask. Without the ability to be slightly funny fairly often, I fear whom I'll discover. Unamusing is unlikeable.

All this mesmerising talk of (and orange hijab woman's unabashed shouting about) mimosa and its cultural significance is beyond the tattooed Spanish woman, and she asks for clarification. Almut, miming a small bush, explains that mimosa is a yellow plant. Almut does a lot of miming – oh if only she were good at it. But orange hijab woman's immediately on the attack again. She'll admit mimosa's yellow, but it's no small bush. No no no, mimosa is a large tree. Almut insists it's small and shrub-like. Orange hijab woman swears it's enormous. And so on and so on, until someone suggests that perhaps, for climatic reasons, mimosa is a small bush in Germany and a large tree in Tunisia.

On a slightly related point, curly-haired Cuban Mira demands to know why all trees in Berlin have numbers. It's true, they do – all four hundred and forty thousand of them are tagged. In fact, Berlin's tree bureaucrats are fanatics. Perhaps it's a legacy of the period when the urban island of West Berlin felt itself painfully detached from the woods. It's also no doubt to do with the centuries before that, when the forests were of profound importance in shaping what Germans were and are. Inured to this, Almut fails to grasp that numbering trees might seem strange to someone from an island ninety per cent of which is covered by dense vegetation, and she has no answer to Mira's question. I suspect that, even if there were no historical motive, Berliners would still number trees. Many I've met fetishize classification of one sort or another. I live with a man who organises his DVDs alphabetically according to director and stores towels in line with Klimt's colour palate.

The unalloyed joy of learning hasn't lasted long. Confident as I am leading a company of actors in a rehearsal room, the last few days have taught me how negative and mean I can be when I'm out of my comfort zone. I judge my classmates harshly and find most of them wanting. What is it about Joo, for example, that irritates me so? Perhaps it's my age; I'm surrounded by too much youth. For the sake of my future, I know I'm doing the right thing, being here and learning German. But her incessant doodling and noisy stationery is a persistent reminder that I'm in a classroom surrounded by children, forcing me to question whether I shouldn't be doing something a bit more...well, adult. I begin to hate the system in which mastery of the dative is the chief qualification for citizenship.

Invading my space at this very moment is a fat plastic envelope bulging with Xiu's coloured pens. Like her sticker packet, it's got a gummy edge that fastens with a crackling whisper, and it'll take months of fixing and unfixing before the damned thing stops being adhesive. She's evidently unwilling to expose the pens to any unnecessary air or light, so there's a festival of unsticking and sticking back up again as she removes and replaces a red one for feminine, blue for masculine and green for neutral, and the rumpus continues without cease throughout class.

On the plus side, Carola's super friendly with me today, and by break time, even Mervyn's softened. As the three of us set off for the coffee shop, he reveals how his astonishing jumper is uniquely dysfunctional. The front is purple alpaca and the back pink nylon. So your back freezes in the winter and your front roasts in the summer. Stupid but pretty. The jumper, I mean. I'm just thinking that coffee with these two is guaranteed to be Brexit-free, and what a pleasure that will be, when Mervyn starts talking about Boris Johnson.

The great Tory man-child was the mayor when Mervyn worked as a clothes-buyer in London, so he knows a thing or two about him. He's seen an old clip online in which Johnson makes an eloquent case for Turkey's membership of the EU. So why, Mervyn demands to know, is he now threatening the Brits with the idea of Turkish membership, and the consequent migration of seventy-six million Muslims into Britain?

It's a very good question, and I have a very good answer: amorality, self-interest and opportunism. But the Estonian blond doesn't want to listen. He wishes to answer the question himself, which he does by asserting that there shouldn't be a referendum at all. The Brits would be fools to vote for anything other than Remain, and there can be no further discussion on the subject. So there isn't. Instead, we segue into the topic he loves best – accessories. He makes Carola tell us how she came by the snazzy Blancpain watch currently encircling her pretty wrist.

Talk about an unreliable narrator! On closer inspection, I realise that her contact lenses aren't tan coloured at all. The truth is she boasts amazingly beautiful eyes: light blue and sea green with intense brown flecks. Where did I get tan from? I was right about her hair though. It's flaky and straightened (with issues), though it looks less tortured than before. Coffees in hand, and with Mervyn in tow, we step out of the shop and into the sunshine, whereupon I realise I was wrong about her age too. She's not as young as I'd thought.

Golden sandals are the full stop to a tremendously fashionable summer outfit that hugs her sumptuously curvy figure. She wears two medallions round her neck. Both comprise letters strung together. One is her name, and I notice it's spelled Karole, not Carola. The other reads 'TWERK'. Correctly-spelled-Karole confidently owns her height – it's similar to Mervyn's, and he's huge! In fact, she and he seem like super-people compared to the rest of the class, especially to short-arses like me and the less well-washed ones, such as Roberto and the tiddly, tattooed Spanish vegans. Leggy style queens, they remind me of Sally Bowles and the Christopher Isherwood character from Cabaret – impossibly glamorous, at least in the movie version. Which would, (if things continue in so jolly a fashion and we become a regular coffee-time threesome), make me boring old Uncle Max. No, wait. It's Maximilian in 'Cabaret', isn't it? Boring old Uncle Max is in 'The Sound of Music'. Hollywood renderings of Nazi history whirl unhelpfully around my brain. I'm getting ahead of myself. We're just having coffee. Calm down.

In Christopher Isherwood's book, *Goodbye to Berlin,* the Novak family lived on this street, Wassertorstraße. One of the author's own Berlin addresses, Simeonstraße, was just round the corner, although the entire road has since disappeared. In the book, Isherwood describes a large stone archway on Wassertorstraße "daubed with hammers and sickles and Nazi crosses and plastered with tattered bills which advertised auctions or crimes...a deeply shabby cobbled street, littered with sprawling children in tears. And at the end of it, like a tall, dangerously sharp, red instrument, stood a church". Well, the church was destroyed in the war and the stone arch has vanished, along with the cobbles and the political insignia. And what had been a poor white slum is home these days to a large chunk of Berlin's two hundred thousand Turks – and the place where Karole from Botswana (via LA, New York and

Learning German (badly)

Manchester), Mervyn from Estonia, and me from Teddington in Middlesex chat together and drink coffee out of paper cups in the early summer sunshine.

Back in class, Almut produces a small object from her bag. It's the size and shape of a cricket ball but knitted in a kind of sad aubergine colour. As we drill a particular point (with a question and answer format to elicit dative-agreed indefinite articles) Almut poses a question while throwing the ball to a student. The student catches it, responds appropriately, poses a similar question to another classmate and lobs the ball to her, and so on. I find this kind of thing desperately irritating, if not (and I'm not exaggerating) frightening. My reaction to any kind of ball game has always been to run away. People imagine that actors enjoy flinging beanbags around as a kind of trust exercise or warm up, but I promise you, no bean bag's ever been a feature of any of my rehearsals, and I'm praying that Almut's ball isn't hurled my way. Summoning up the correct indefinite article while catching a soft ball when you're behind a table, tight up against people you don't know well, is stressful. There's no space for flailing arms, and several of the Marias are rubbish shots. It turns out, however, that hefty Fairuz (the older of the Arabic ladies) is even less comfortable than I am. A reflex reaction makes her snatch the ball out of the air when it's chucked her way, but she immediately drops it on the floor and wipes her hands, demanding to know from Almut whether it's clean or if dogs have been playing with it. Literally, that's what she says. When it's my turn, I simply pass it to the person next to me. Even better, when it flies towards Karole, she ducks. Each time a catch is muffed, it takes ages to retrieve the ball from among the bags by our feet. A water bottle gets knocked over. Orange hijab woman strikes Jang-Mi on the head. And whenever it takes to the air – literally every single time – girls giggle nervously. The whole thing's ridiculous.

After handing out sheets of song lyrics, Almut plays us a track from an old audiocassette. Doing nothing for my self-esteem, Mervyn excitedly announces that he's seen pictures of cassette players online but never actually heard one play anything. The track's a show-tune from '*Linie Eins*' ('Line One'), a West Berlin rock musical from the '80s, the title referring to the subway line that runs along the elevated tracks east and west by our school. Songs can be a useful way of introducing new vocabulary, but I'm barely able to follow the lyrics through nostalgic tears. It's not so much the song itself I'm moved by – a big-haired, theatrical ballad – as the setting and the time: Bahnhof Zoo in the days of the divided city.

During the Cold War, Zoo Station functioned as West Berlin's main railway terminus and was a mecca for the city's demi-monde. So the music transports me back to a seedily sensuous world of graffiti, dingy anarchic clubs, Christiane F and sex'n'drugs'n'rock'n'roll among the ruins of war. Decades peel away and formative moments of my youth flash before me. But I'm not recalling Zoo Station in the '70s because I lived in Berlin in those days, and encountered the rent boys and the junkies. I didn't. I'm remembering films I've seen which describe that time and which moved me. I was in Bahnhof Zoo in the '80s only in as much as I owned albums by Bowie and U2 that were inspired by it and gave me a sensation of connection. I'm nostalgic for something I've never experienced. And yet the Wall that divided a nation, along with the political posturing around Checkpoint Charlie that for decades impacted way beyond the city, were all a part of my youth.

These days, the threat of Brexit provides me with a much more concrete reason to be interested in a divided nation, so, when Almut announces that she intends to organise a class outing to see the show live, I'm the first to sign up.

Learning German (badly)

I spend a challenging afternoon with *Emma*. Over the last couple of days I've taken the drastic step of trying to map out her story without reference to marriage, but, once I get Mr Elton and Miss Bates up to the top of Box Hill, I see that the approach is nonsense. Marriage is what it's all about. Clearly, there's nothing to be gained by fucking about with Austen's narrative. If you don't follow her faithfully, she'll make your life hell. Yet, I feel duty bound to find some contemporary relevance in the adaptation, to synthesise the best of Austen and a twist of now, to express what this classic means to me and share it with an audience. But at the moment, I still can't see a clear way through. When Sven returns from work, I'm happy to close down Word and help him with dinner.

As we stand at the kitchen counter peeling asparagus together, I explain how shocked I was that Korean man sat next to me today, but Sven's unimpressed. He suggests the guy must feel embarrassed for me because of the way I excluded myself so defiantly over the birthday cake. The pain that he felt on my behalf will have been ameliorated by sitting next to me. It's a chance to use another one of those splendid compound nouns – *Fremdschämen* – the feeling of being ashamed on someone else's behalf. The understanding of others. The root of kindness.

...

After dinner, I bike over to visit our lovely friend Bettina. She often invites me to study introductory-level German literature with her – a poem or something. To me, these evenings are not only incredibly helpful but also utterly pleasurable. Lesbian and socialist, she's around my age, and has been an academic. Now she edits film and volunteers her spare time to teach German to Syrian refugees. Though she's the opposite of a namedropper, her mother was an actress, and she does have a sliver of a story about Bertolt Brecht to tell me before we start translating one of his poems.

Her mum was never particularly successful and, even before Bettina was born, she'd given up acting to become a full-time wife and mother, but while she was still striving for success in the theatre, she and her actor-boyfriend were visited in their apartment by the great man himself, who, unannounced, pitched up in the company of Ruth Berlau, his collaborator and lover. Bettina's mum was so in awe that she refused to come out of the kitchen, and remained there, chain-smoking with Berlau, while Brecht talked to her boyfriend in the drawing room. Even when the famous pair bade her farewell, she couldn't utter a sound, but shortly after his departure, she spotted his pipe. She grabbed it, raced outside, and, unsure which way he'd gone, sprinted down the road shouting "Herr Brecht, your pipe! Your pipe, Herr Brecht!"

I don't know why I like the story so much. It's something to do with the smallness of it, I suppose. It was an utterly forgettable non-event for Brecht, I dare say, but it was huge for Bettina's Mum. And there's something touching about her reckless flight, as if she's chasing a dream she knew would never materialise.

Bettina's patience and gentle encouragement persuade me to broach material I'd normally have thought impossible. Her generosity and Brecht's genius restore a little of my lost faith in the arduous process of getting German under my belt, and I'm reminded that if I persist, the rewards are there for the taking.

The poem we study is about a cloud. It speaks of memory – how your mind doggedly clings to the irrelevant details. You don't remember the kiss, Brecht writes, beyond the mundane fact that there was one. What you remember is the cloud that sat in the sky above you. *Ungeheuer oben*. Terribly high above.

Back home again, I see I've missed a call from Mum, so I phone her back to hear that Dad's gone into hospital. This morning's check-up revealed his liver levels were worryingly out of kilter, and the doctor called for an ambulance to take him straight in. Dad asked if he could go home and pack some things and drive himself there tomorrow, but the doctor said there might not be a tomorrow for him if he didn't do what he was told. Mum's in shock, Dad's in shock. While no one knows anything for certain, all we can do is agree to talk again in the morning.

Friday 10th June

There's no information from home because Mum can't get through to the nurse's station on Dad's ward, and visiting hours don't start until after lunch.

Referendum news is equally discouraging. Over breakfast, I watch another TV debate on catch-up through my shonky VPN. This time, Tory Remainers take the opportunity to write Johnson off as a liar, a drunk and a man motivated exclusively by personal ambition. Tory MP Amber Rudd even announces that he's "the life and soul of the party but not the man you want driving you home at the end of the evening". It's a pretty grizzly state of affairs when you find yourself admiring Amber Rudd.

I'm amazed how grubby the tone of the debate is. Well, debate is hardly the word. It's a top-down, personality-based shambles guaranteeing that the public remains in the dark about the real issues. The Leavers fan the fire of people's fear of foreigners, and Remainers stick to economics without contributing any historical perspective, big dream or proper defence of the European idea. Rudd and chums appear incapable of persuading an undecided nation to vote Remain, and they look as rattled and jumpy as I feel.

I've learned a lot about powerlessness. I know that anxiety is useless – it helps no one and doesn't diminish the source of my worry. But I can no longer quash my raging disquiet with a quick recitation of the serenity prayer. Uneasiness spreads into every nook and cranny of thinking because the ramifications of a potential Brexit are so incalculably huge. I tell myself, for the billionth time, just go to class, work on *Emma* and apply for citizenship, then you're covered whatever happens. But the 'what if' chorus won't be stilled. It starts like a whisper and spirals into a shrieking tinnitus, threatening my concentration and skewing my drive. What if you fail the course? What if you get one of those awkward bastards who doesn't like the cut of your jib and turns down your application for citizenship on a whim? What if Leave wins and your EU health insurance becomes invalid? What if you never get another job and they deport you and you run out of money and you starve to death and... Most of it's illogical, and all of it's hysterical, but logic is powerless in the face of this level of unpredictability.

In class, however, all is sunshine. After two days away, Roberto's back, smelling of bacon and cigarettes, though I'm not sure Almut's so thrilled. She openly laughs at him when he gets something wrong. That can't be good pedagogy, surely? For all the glamour of Karole and Mervyn, if Roberto liked me I'd be satisfied. He's a salt-of-the-earth washer-upperer who may not be 'the brightest light in the harbour' as the Germans would say, but he studies hard, is always willing to have a go, and manages to maintain dogged cheerfulness in the face of Almut's patronising underestimation of him. I think he's great.

Just before the break, his girlfriend bursts into the room, bearing an enormous box full of homemade muffins, filling the place with a heavenly fresh-baked smell and waving to her friends. The group knows her because she also attends the VHS, though at Advanced level, and Almut welcomes her as if it were a perfectly natural thing to do. But is it? I'm infuriated by this fresh waste of time. Unless we're fully focussed on learning, my anxiety tinnitus has a habit of kicking in and drowning out German instruction. But Francesca won't be drowned out. Like Roberto, she hails from Sicily and, with her enormous teeth, thick glasses and double chin, she's the most affable girl in the world. She works as a dinner lady in a kindergarten, so you see what can be achieved with Advanced German.

I hang around because I'm keen for her to know that I'm only turning down her offer of a muffin due to my gluten intolerance, and then I spend the rest of the break with Karole, Mervyn and a Maria I've yet to get to talk to properly: pretty Brazilian Melina.

Boasting excellent English and super-snazzy sunglasses, she runs counter to my *idée fixe* that all Brazilians are effervescent creatures in thrall to dancing and shagging. In fact, she sounds dourly defeated as she moans about a job she went for and didn't get. Perhaps it might have helped, I muse, if she opened her mouth a bit when speaking. I feel like the irritated director I can sometimes be. "AR-TIC-U-LATE!" I long to yell. Instead, I politely ask her what she does for work, aware that the question poses conversational risk. As with Francesca, what people do in Berlin is not necessarily what they did where they come from, and the disjuncture, when light is shone on it, can hurt. Roberto worked in catering before qualifying as an archaeologist in Palermo, and now finds himself back in catering again, washing up in a restaurant, though he seems entirely cheerful about it. In Melina's case, having been an engineer on a perfectly decent salary in Salvador, she's currently unemployed and needs someone to buy her a coffee. And she isn't cheerful about it at all.

Since his glamorous London days when he lived in Knightsbridge and earned shed-loads of dosh as a buyer for Harrods, Mervyn confesses that, now he's in Berlin, he "isn't anything". But at least he's keeping his sartorial standards up. Though it's about twenty-nine degrees, today's outfit includes a thick white woollen jacket with comically huge buttons, faded denim short shorts and what I think are called deck shoes. He wears no socks and I notice his thick ankles. Karole is also between jobs, but says she'd like to be a health manager, which apparently is a kind of cross between a nutritionist and a lifestyle coach. She explains it all to me at great, no, at encyclopaedic length. Note to self: I must stop judging these people as if they're only here to amuse me.

It's as if Almut's read our minds because, back in class, she wishes us to discuss employment in order to practise the conditional. After being split into pairs, we must quiz our partner about the kind of employment conditions we look for ('Would you travel for work?', 'Would you work outdoors?' etc). I'm paired with Irish Tracey, but when I ask her the questions, she struggles with the answers, and when it's her turn with the questions, she can't do them either.

As is often the case, Almut opts for a general chat. These are always a challenge for me because it's invariably the same people who are 'keen to add their mustard' as the Germans say. Opinions are predictable and conflicts are inevitable, and while the least talented and least interesting students hog the discourse, my 'what if Brexit' chorus gets out its brass instruments and starts up a military march. Curly-haired Cuban Mira will become aerated and loud, flick her hair for emphasis, flick, flick, flick, and go off on a monologue about what a giant her brother is or how she once only narrowly avoided being abducted into the slave trade. Tracey will offer some left-field nonsense about leprechauns or the luck of the Irish, and orange hijab woman will behave as if the whole thing's a private conversation class organised exclusively for her. This time, an argument erupts about what exactly the differences are between trial jobs, mini-jobs, part-time jobs, half-day jobs, temporary jobs, black jobs, job share and internships, i.e. the sorts of jobs people like us are most likely to get. Cuban Mira reports that her boss has got all handsy and is a perv.

Almut encourages us to fantasize about our dream job, and thus we discover that, in Roberto's ideal world, he drives a *Straßenbahn* (a tram) around Berlin. There's no mention of archaeology. It's all about the trams. To demonstrate, he leans back, spreads his legs, rests one arm on an imaginary steering wheel and spins it, left and right, like a relaxed 1950s Formula One driver slaloming through an undemanding chicane, until Almut points out that trams in Berlin run on tracks in straight lines. There's no steering involved. "There is in my mind," Roberto mutters.

As for myself, I'm already doing my dream job, but I don't wish to admit that to the class for fear of sounding smug. It appears that most people don't have any grand ideas about what they'd like to do with their lives. They don't dream about jobs. Living in Berlin is enough.

One of the most infuriating aspects of my Brexit-related anxiety is that I quite patently have no reason to be anxious. The UK hasn't voted to leave the EU. I have a lovely life in Berlin. I have the job I want. I'm in love with my boyfriend. What the hell have I got to complain about? I am no Cassandra. Of all the people I know, I genuinely have one of the sunniest dispositions, but while the clouds gather above, I can feel something moving under the rocks below. I'm aware my prognosis is hardly scientific, but this good life is under threat. I know it.

Our instructress needs to spend a part of every class on German culture, and so she moves us onto the subject of *Vereine* (clubs). This seems a bit abstruse, until we're told the club has a special status in German society, since like-mindedness and community spirit are especially prized here. I'm happy to learn about it, because the way groups work here and the responsibility they take for themselves are two of the reasons I choose Germany over England.

Famously, Berliners are far from compliant, but they are law-abiding. Yes, they're often brusque, but they're respectful of others and averse to anti-social behaviour. It was a terrible shock to the foreign students who live opposite me when the police came round and instructed them to pack up their party when it became noisy after ten p.m. They'd assumed that Berlin means liberation from everything, including the need to think about others.

Our interfering neighbour is an obvious case in point. If you misbehave in the house (for example, by putting the wrong trash in the wrong bin, or, in the Libyans' case, by holding tea parties in the cellar), your neighbour will not hesitate to let you know as brusquely as she thinks necessary. But, by the same token, if anyone requires help or support, they can be sure to get it from those who live close-by. It's all part of the notion of the group taking care of itself.

In terms of communitarian living, once you've spent a year or so here, you can't help but notice that this quaint notion impacts on the quality of life in all sorts of lovely ways. Berlin feels a lot more neighbourhoody than London, and the neighbourhood (*Kiez*) is a concept key to the German's understanding of urban living. *Kiez* means more to a German than just neighbourhood, partly because of the way urban accommodation has developed. People live together in houses, rarely in anonymous blocks.

I saw a flyer in our local tailor's shop on Oranienstraße that aimed to inspire the neighbourhood to defend itself against gentrification. It defined *Kiez*, whether it's a block or just a section of a street, as 'neighbours who know each other, stick together and stand up for each other'. The neighbourhood, according to the leaflet, is characterised by 'long nights of talk, drink and dance, but also respect for those who have to get up early in the morning'. And life operates for many on this level.

As a pedestrian, you wait for the famous little green walking man in his traffic light before you cross the road. Even if no car is in sight, you wait, otherwise a fellow citizen will most likely yell at you about setting a bad example for the children. Now summer is upon us, you can bike to the park, but you will behave with respect. Children aren't screaming and no one's playing music too loudly. Everyone does what they want and enjoys themselves, but at the same time you can relax, because parks are not places where the rules of civilisation are abandoned.

Church bells ring at the drop of a hat. You can't buy anything on a Sunday. Friday finishes early and free time is free time. Once office hours are over, you stop work. I've never seen a self-service check-out machine in a Berlin supermarket. Yes, it takes a bit longer to pay for your groceries, but none of the staff has lost jobs. Neoliberalism hasn't succeeded in demolishing worker's rights, despite Chancellor Schröder's turn-of-the-millennium labour-bashing reforms.

Perhaps my final example of social self-nurturing is silly, but it was one that astonished me above all others: When a German man enters the changing room at the gym, he will greet his fellows. In London, if you stride about the gym saying hello to strangers, they'll think your mad, foreign or gay.

I should add that many things pull against this idyll of communal living I enjoy describing. Perhaps most notably is the neighbourhood army I mentioned earlier, the ones responsible for distributing leaflets about the importance of the *Kiez*. Their MO is to gather at night and destroy any plucky bud of modernisation that might have broken ground locally; although their methods are violent, you could argue that even their action is within the spirit of neighbourly cohesion. Berlin is changing fast, and growth means that some of the old working-class *Kieze* are becoming unrecognisable. In response, this self-appointed band of punks and anarchists believe they're protecting the place for the ordinary inhabitants by attempting to reverse the process. It's all great fun and very Berlinish, but they will insist on continually smashing up the new furniture shop on the corner of our street, which is a great shame as we really like the people who run it, and we bought a lovely sofa from them quite recently. But as fast as the windows are repaired, the mob emerges in the middle of the night and shatters them all over again.

As we head for our bikes after class, Korean man waylays me. His name is Woong, and he wonders if I'd be kind enough to peruse a letter he's received from his electricity provider. He thinks it requires him to do something, but he doesn't know what. Unfortunately, there are too many words on the damned thing that mean nothing to me, or to Roberto who comes to our aid. We suggest he asks Almut about it, and he agrees that he will, but he doesn't. Being Asian, he's too in awe of his teacher to bother her with a mere utility bill. His partner, Jang-Mi, who wears a fetching, floppy summer hat, invites us all to a picnic in the park on Saturday. She promises her cat will be there.

Her cat is called Woojoo.

Woojoo is Korean for universe.

...

This evening, the Euros kick off at the *Stade de France* in St Denis, where the home team take on Romania. I'm so sorry for Dad that he's going to miss it. He'll be incredibly pissed off. Before other plans emerged, there was a suggestion that Sven and I should stay in to watch, or else go see it on a screen somewhere in town, an activity for which the Germans insist on borrowing the English words, *Public Viewing*.

To my mind, 'public viewing' conjures up a memory of the viewing gallery where, as a child in the '60s, I used to watch Dad play squash in the Tolworth Recreation Centre. But for Germans, who, when sequestering English words, often get them slightly wrong, it's all about drinking and community and watching sport in the sunshine.

Although the so-called Beautiful Game attracts if not generates thuggery, racism, sexism and homophobia, there's something about a pan-European competition of any sort that hooks me in. Likewise for Sven. It's one of the reasons we're both nuts about the Eurovision Song Contest. It's like war, but safer and sublimated. It intrigues me to observe recognizable national traits replicated in different international arenas. Britain's fixation with past glories and an overblown sense of its own uniqueness is as visible at meetings of the European Council ("Rebate!" "Opt out!") as it is during Eurovision, for which it would be distasteful to try hard. We just submit terrible songs, complain about bloc voting and yell 'foul' when we don't claim the prize every year. Same with the footie: What other country would feel entitled to deploy four distinct football teams? How would the English feel if Germany sent a national team to the Euros backed up by additional ones from Mecklenburg-Vorpommern, North Rhein-Westphalia and Saxony-Anhalt? Nevertheless, the competition in itself is a marvellous thing and we intend to catch as much of it as possible. The notion of tiny Iceland competing against the big boys is especially thrilling, and reminds me of Luxembourg's honourable history in Eurovision, which it won three times ('65, '72 and '73), despite running out of its own singers quite early on, and long before Germany had won it once.

Decades after France and England stretched to a bit of ethnic diversity in their soccer teams, Germany finally fields one for the Euros that reflects its population. At last, the *Deutsche Mannschaft* will include a bunch of foreign-born players, including a Pole, a Turk and a Tunisian. Paradoxically, when it comes to Eurovision, it's traditionally been the entrant most likely to send foreigners to represent it. In the first twenty years of the contest's history, West Germany submitted a Pole, a Bulgarian, a Swede, a Dane, a Norwegian, an Austrian and a Brit. I guess the thinking went that it would be hard for anyone to vote for a German so soon after the war. It was a case of having to construct a new identity. 'Who are we?', the West Germans spent much of the first twenty-five post-war years wondering. In fact, it wasn't until 1982, the year when they elected sixteen-year-old Nicole to sing for them, that they stood a chance of doing well. She was pretty, blond and so young that she couldn't feasibly have had anything to do with the Holocaust. She sung a sweet ditty about peace and swept the board.

There'll be no footie for Sven and me tonight because he's accepted an invitation to a *Vernissage* (exhibition opening) in Prenzlauer Berg, and friend-of-a-friend Aaron has phoned me out of the blue to ask me out for a drink. Aaron's a fellow ex-pat writer who I've been trying to pin down for ages so we can have a chat about our mutually-related projects.

He moved from Australia only a couple of years ago, but as we order Aperol spritzes he tells me that not only has he got himself work as a regular contributor to the English language section of Berlin's monthly gay magazine '*Siegessäule*', but he's also finished penning an essential new guide to the city's club scene for which he's found a publisher. I've lived here twice as long, and haven't achieved half as much. But then, Aaron's altogether awe-inspiring.

While we wait for our drinks at the bar, we share our bafflement about Brexit. Magical thinking would have me believe that I can prevent disaster if I constantly refer to the threat of it, but tonight's not the night for referendum talk. I'm not here to make Aaron understand the urgent concerns of every Brit in Europe. I'm here for work, and as soon as we sit down, it's apparent it won't be a challenge to get him to discuss his speciality with me. He revels in describing the adventures he's had in the cause of researching his new book, painting a picture of the city with impressive gusto and hardly taking a breath.

He's especially interested in Berlin's more decadent dives where he does most of his research, and the tales of his sexual capers remind me that the city I once loved as a tourist is no longer the town I currently inhabit. In those days, as an occasional visitor, I'd feel as comfortable in 'Lab', the remarkable sex club that nestles underneath Berghain, as I would in the great national museums on the *Museumsinsel*. In other words, Berlin is large enough to contain diverse worlds. You can get lost in one and forget that the others even exist. Though my crusade of sexual discovery is over, for Aaron and the many visitors who come primarily for the parties and clubs, this city is, as it was eighty years ago, the world capital of decadence. And indeed, there's plenty of it, if you know where to look.

On Köpenicker Straße, around the corner from our apartment, sits the celebrated 'KitKatClub' which hosts a monthly 'direct-action enterprise' called *FickstutenMarkt*. This might be translated as 'horse fair', though *fick* also means fuck. There are copycat events in other cities, but Berlin's is the original. The place is decked out with scaffolding, slings and black-PVC-covered mattresses, with the less exposed areas reserved for the 'shyer animals'. If you fancy yourself as a 'mare' you turn up early to be given a bag that you wear over your head throughout the evening – white if you elect to have safe sex and red if not – after which you're tied to a post. Later on, the stallions arrive, and Bob's your uncle Fanny's your – well, you get the idea. Bacchanalian, yes, but, this being Berlin, it's meticulously well-organised too, so dissipation never degenerates into chaos. Staff dressed as horse trainers circulate with flashlights to ensure that sex remains safe for those who've opted for it. Mares are allowed to take breaks or go home when they've had enough. At the end of the night, prizes are awarded.

If you want to have anonymous sex with another man at eight o'clock on a midweek morning, head to Schöneberg and clubs such as the seedy Bull or otherworldly New Action. If you wish to see gay men decked out in leather being led about the street like dogs, go to Motzstraße during Folsom weekend, or on almost any Saturday night to tell the truth. During the summer you can hardly move for annual gay street events. The parade on Christopher Street Day is the main one, but there's also a leather one, a bondage one, and all sorts of other ones. In fact, there's tons of action of every sort citywide to underpin the capital's reputation as the place to be for a barrier-busting sexual spree.

And that status will probably exist as long as Berlin continues to attract international migrants, misfits and global partygoers. I see it as a manifestation of the place's on-going spirit of anarchic protest and its glorification of freedom, which continues to burn brightly more than a quarter of a century after the fall of the wall. Berlin's party ethos is a testament to what the city's meant to millions of people for hundreds of years, as well as what it stands for today: an island of hope and tenacity; peoples' inexorable impulse to live in the face of catastrophe; their adamantine insistence that life must be celebrated, especially when it often proves to be so fragile and short.

Learning German (badly)

To my mind, London and Paris are organised for the benefit of an elite, ill disposed towards the idea that the workers have to live there as well as work. Egalitarian and pluralist Berlin, conversely, is the product of practical and unexciting social democracy in action. The trains and buses are comfortable and they run punctually and consistently. Employers cooperate with trade unions to nurture employees. There's always somewhere to spend time for free if you're without work. The elected representatives look like ordinary humans, not Edwardian stiffs. The system that integrates the refugees, though flawed, tries its best to be kind. An impressive network of *Schwulenberatung* (queer counselling centres and social clubs) help young gay people find their feet. In the Schöneberg district, there's a police station populated entirely by LGBT staff.

If London's a messy drunk who blanks out and does destructive things, Berlin's an occasional heavy drinker who never loses control.

I should say that, when I talk like this, Sven reminds me that I'm utterly ignorant of the many white trash districts where some of the above might not pertain. Like any group of people, Berliners, let alone Germans, fiercely resist categorization: wildly exuberant one moment, philosophical the next, capable of brutal honesty and mawkish sentimentality. Famous for their efficiency, I find them averagely inefficient. Infamous for their lack of a sense of humour, it seems to me they make jokes and laugh as frequently as anybody else. There are as many brilliant and stupid Germans as there are brilliant and stupid people anywhere else.

But one thing everyone can agree on is that the German people are experts at regulation and red tape. While their scrupulous attention to the detail of the document usually ensures a high degree of smoothness and legality, it can sometimes create a vicious snarl entangling those it's designed to assist. Last month, a report detailed how a Chinese tourist had his wallet stolen while on holiday in Karlsruhe and, after he'd signed the wrong piece of paper in the police station, ended up in a refugee camp for two weeks. It wasn't until the centre's officials asked workers in a nearby Chinese restaurant to interpret for them that he was released from his involuntary asylum. Manager Herr Schlütermann remarked that the thirty-one-year-old Chinese man had "set machinery in motion that he couldn't get out of."

Shouldn't this Kafkaesque nightmare be made into a movie? I'm tempted to bash out a screenplay. Before Aaron does.

Saturday 11th June

False alarm. They're keeping Dad under observation for a further couple of days, but if all goes well, they hope to have him home by Tuesday. The trouble is that the pills for his heart strain his liver, and the pills for his liver strain his heart, and whenever anything goes out of whack, his psoriasis flairs up. So there's a lot to contend with, but apparently everything's now back within a normal operating window. So he's delighted, and so is Mum, that he appears to be on the mend, and he can get home and watch some football. No one however, is prepared to say whether our trip to see them next weekend should be postponed.

The last time Sven and I paid a visit, just before Christmas, the old man was looking tired, and older than ever. He wasn't as engaged as usual and, over lunch, fell asleep in the middle of a sentence. So these new developments are hardly shocking. He's getting on for ninety, so stuff is bound to go wrong. But mentally he's all there, and I've no doubt there's plenty more life in him yet.

...

With nothing but sunshine predicted for the weekend, we set off on our bikes for the first proper ride of the season. Cycling east, skirting the route of the old wall, racing away from our home district of Kreuzberg, we quickly reach Treptow Park, where the towering larkspurs blaze blue and purple, and our foreheads and noses turn fluorescent pink. We follow the River Spree, bristling with red and white boats bobbing about in the dazzling sunshine, and in the cool of the shade under the waterside trees, find ourselves pedalling out of town, tracing the edge of Plänterwald, an East German-built theme park that fell into disrepair after the Wall fell, but has never been properly dismantled. The rotting roller coaster is enfolded by leafy branches, and gargantuan dinosaurs lie on their sides, red with rust, powerless against the remorseless advance of vegetation, their hollowness revealed.

By early evening, we're back in town. We've got tickets for the theatre this evening so, after tons of sun cream has been applied, we pitch up at the Volksbühne (The Peoples' Stage) on Rosa-Luxemburg-Platz to see the show. The Volksbühne's one of Berlin's most legendary spaces, and the city's tumultuous history is woven into the fabric of the building. Founded with the express purpose of bringing art to the working class, its radical, anti-capitalist, avant-garde repertoire has won it an international reputation.

In many of Berlin's larger houses, theatre performances are surtitled, and if Sven and I are looking to be entertained, and surtitles are not available, we often prefer to see a dance piece, or watch a movie in English. But I try to keep abreast of what's going on in the theatre whether I understand all the words or not, and in this case an artist friend has co-curated the show, so we feel obliged to see what he's wrought. As you can probably tell from the word 'co-curated', we are not in for a traditional play.

Fabled theatre director Frank Castorf has run the Volksbühne since Unification, but this is the last season he's programming. Apart from his stint as artistic director in Rosa-Luxemburg-Platz, he's renowned for developing what's called 'post-dramatic theatre', his 2013 production of the Ring Cycle at Bayreuth being a stand-out example of the form. While it left everyone bemused, if not scared and angry, in his defence Castorf said that he'd meant it to be incomprehensible.

What has always been the most recognisable feature of his productions is what I call the 'Castorf slow death moment'. With a nod to Pinter's notion of the pause, as well as an acknowledgment of ideas around repetition and playing with time, it's a prominent part of his armoury. Now widely copied throughout the land, it can involve any piece of stage business, though preferably something already small, slow and mundane, which, under his direction, just goes on and on for ages – ages and ages and ages – beyond all sense of conventional story-telling or theatrical pace. It's either a single thing done death-defyingly slowly, or a normal thing repeated *ad nauseum*. Witnessing an example of it is a bit like watching a glacier move, but without the grandeur or the relevance. As the suspension of disbelief evaporates, you arrive at a weary acceptance that the director is exploring an intellectual idea, or 'having a wank' as we say in the theatre, and, in a kind of stupor in which you have plenty of time to examine your desire for oblivion, it might suddenly occur to you that you've paid to see this shit and voluntarily dedicated your evening to culture, when you could have been down the pub or watching the telly for free. When Alfred Hitchcock asked, "What is drama but life with the dull bits cut out?", Castorf's answer was to direct productions full of dull bits with the life cut out.

Anyway, the thing we're seeing tonight is not by Carstorf. It's something he's programmed. And though it's taking place very much inside a theatre, with a stage and an auditorium and everything, there is no text. There are no live actors. Instead, what we get are several unrelated installations featuring painting (unremarkable), soundscapes (drony), slowly revolving rooms you can enter (been there, done that), and bits of video (bad). The latter comprises re-enacted scenes stolen from the film 'Rebel Without A Cause', performed by atrocious actors in shocking wigs (one assumes intentionally so), and there's heaps of nudity. We're definitely meant to be shocked but, judging from people's faces, no one is, because it takes more than a flash of cock to ruffle a Berliner.

As the season brochure puts it (in English), with typically effusive waffle, no aversion to repetition and little grip of punctuation, 'The project wishes to explore how the fine arts and theatre mutually influence one another and to generate synergistic effects for both genres through new aesthetic inspiration from the fine arts – with the aim of exploring the political relevance of art utopias of the 1960s in our current socio-political situation.'

Enervated to the level that only bad theatre can take you, Sven and I head for the bar, and, after two lovely *Grauburgunders*, decide that what we really want to do is go home and watch Friends on DVD.

Sunday 12th June

As predicted, the amazing weather continues without cease, so we spend the entire morning on the terrace reading, rehashing last night's theatre and trying not to worry too much about either Brexit or Dad.

When Sven suggests I should fret less, I point out that he possesses all the security he needs: a permanent job, comprehensive medical insurance he can afford, and citizenship of a country that, for the same reason it joined the EU, is the least likely to abandon it. My uncertainly is as much to do with the fact of my being a freelancer as it is about my being a Brit. Nothing about German citizenship comes cheap. It brings obligations as well as perks. Mandatory medical insurance that costs hundreds a month is the least of it. Living in Germany inevitably diminishes my job prospects in England. My income source is far from guaranteed. I've supported myself for decades, and I don't want to start living off anyone else now. Not to mention, if it wasn't for the referendum, I wouldn't be applying for German citizenship. The last thing I want is to define myself nationalistically. And though I love Germany, I wouldn't, in any other circumstances, necessarily elect to become a citizen of a country after living in it for only four years. The threat of Brexit forces me to choose whether to be German or English, when all I want is to remain European. Freedom might be defined as having the right to choose, but if it *obliges* me to make a choice, it's not freedom.

It's clear this tedious, though heartfelt, stew of perturbation is threatening to kill our lovely Sunday, so Sven asks why we shouldn't transcend our workaday worries by visiting some art. Relieved to pack my concerns away for a while, I agree.

The city's not short of artists, especially young ones. The only thing that there's more of is DJs. So the contemporary art community is vast, and the scene extensive and diverse. It's short on buyers, though. In Düsseldorf and Munich, people have cash to splash, but I've never met anyone in Berlin who's managed to survive by art alone.

As inspiration, Berlin provides a cornucopia of thrilling modern art spaces, from the sensational 'me Collectors Room' to the grand Hamburger Bahnhof. Unsurprisingly, the city's Contemporary Biennale is a spectacular affair that's available to be enjoyed in various locations all over town, including a boat-as-installation that chugs you up and down the River Spree. The venue Sven and I pick to begin our artistic odyssey is the European School of Management and Technology, which occupies an impressive 1960s ex-government building in the very centre of town, on Schloßplatz.

Originally the seat of the *Staatsrat* (East Germany's government), the building retains all the trappings of socialist utopian architecture, notably the vast and outrageously colourful stained-glass windows that depict the workers of the world uniting and doing terribly well in lovely conditions. Politically speaking, the present owners – a private, not-for-profit educational facility bankrolled by capitalist corporations – couldn't be more antithetical to the old DDR. To emphasise the point, they've recast the building in English, naming the rooms things like 'The Competence Lounge' and 'The Success Suite' into which disappear sharply dressed young people whose bearing suggests that they have every intention of bossing the future.

Invading these two opposed ideologies throughout the summer is an assembly of contemporary work that concerns itself with questions provoked by the notion of a digital dystopia. The highly-prized and generously-funded pieces represent a dazzling range of artistic responses to digital blue-sky thinking, including a wonky running track, which in its scale and raw physicality, ironically, is very theatrical, and which Sven and I find disturbing (in a good way), and a video about satellite technology, which is harder to engage with. We head back out onto Schloßplatz to reunite with our bikes, musing about what we've seen. At the Volksbühne, it was theatre as installation. Here, it's art as video. The established disciplines collide and merge.

Schloßplatz (the *platz* around the *Schloß* - the palace) has felt the impact of every chapter of Germany's history and has always spoken of the nation's identity – from its early days as a mediaeval military fort surrounded by marshland, to the era when it was home to a succession of Brandenburg electors, Prussian kings and Holy Roman emperors. Today, these epochs sometimes overlap or are superimposed on one another architecturally. Before we cycle away, Sven directs my attention back to the '60s-built structure we've just exited. I hadn't noticed, but stuck on the front of it is an incongruous baroque balcony. He explains that it used to form part of the old *Schloß* that stood on the other side of the road, but, along with the entire portal that surrounded it, it was snatched from the rubble of the bombed palace at the end of the war and preserved by the socialists, not because of its beauty but because of its political significance. From that very balcony, the co-founder of Germany's communist party, Karl Liebknecht, proclaimed the existence of the Free Socialist Republic that terminated Germany's monarchy on November 9th 1918. (Intriguingly, the birth of German socialism is one of several pivotal events that have occurred over the years on November 9th, including Hitler's failed beer hall putsch in 1923, Kristallnacht in '38 and the fall of the Wall in '89. The Germans call it their 'Day of Fate'.)

After the war, the socialists built their prodigiously grand Palace of the Republic where the *Schloß* had stood. That symbol of authoritarianism was in turn erased by Schröder's government after the Wall fell. Currently, the six-hundred-year-old baroque *Schloß* is being given a second lease of life, replicated stone for stone, as yet one more reminder of Prussian Berlin's martial past. I wonder whether the city needs it, especially at its projected cost. But politically, I suppose, it's inevitable. Isn't second-hand mediaeval grandeur the perfect expression of neoliberalism?

Despite Germany's reputation for ruthless efficiency, big projects have a habit of being delayed, especially in Berlin, where nothing involving state money is achievable without scandal and obstruction. The new airport, for instance, which, when you land at Schönefeld you can see, grand and shiny in the distance, has been tantalisingly near its completion for so long that its official opening was announced for 2010, then for 2014, then for 2017, then for 2018. But they just can't quite finish it. They've given up estimating the launch date now. Rumours circulate: The electrics are all wrong, the systems aren't integrated… Whatever. Berliners believe that if it's ever to open, they'll first have to demolish the whole thing and begin all over again.

…

In the evening, it's time for *Sauerbraten*. I'm working my way round German-speaking Gastronomia and am currently in Austria. And what's not to love about a recipe that includes the instruction 'After a week…'?! So seven days after putting a great slab of meat in the fridge to pickle, it's finally ready for braising. And that takes hours. Then it's just the *Rotkohl* and *Kartoffelklöße* to prepare (red cabbage and potato pancakes). Sounds scientific, but mostly they come in tins and packets. Even so, the whole thing is certainly longwinded. But it's not difficult, and what you end up with is gloriously tender meat in a gorgeous silky sauce. I use beef of course, unlike the Rhinelanders who apparently prefer horse.

Monday 13th June

Despite being unable to let go of referendum worries altogether, I found the weekend very centring. I feel refreshed and re-motivated, and determined that, with enough vim and vigour, I can achieve my goal. As we launch ourselves on week two of A-2-2, I'm happy to see my classmates and feel less conspicuously the new boy. I'm not saying I belong to the core of the group yet, for the core went to the park on Saturday with the Koreans and Woojoo the cat.

Almut kicks us off with comparative and superlative adjectives, which is reassuringly easy because last year's Beginner course covered it. Easy, easier, the easiest = *einfach, einfacher, am einfachsten*.

Old, older, the oldest = *alt, älter, am ältesten*.
Karole ist älter als Joo, aber ich bin am ältesten.

Everyone dutifully coughs up something, though Joo of course resists. Our instructress becomes suddenly implacable and, when Joo giggles and refuses to try, things get tense. Under duress, she finally offers "*Die USA ist größer als China, aber China hat mehr Leute*" (The USA's bigger than China, but China has more people). Her face displays grim satisfaction, tinged with hatred, as she scornfully turns back to a scrap of paper on which she's spent the morning doodling chickens.

I can hardly wait for break to hear all about the shenanigans in the park, and as we hit the pavement outside school, I duly learn that Jang-Mi and Woong provided extraordinary amounts of exquisite, authentic Korean food, Woojoo the cat was sheer delight and everyone had a tip-top time. None of the Arab ladies attended.

The tattooed Spanish girl has re-coloured her hair. What was magenta is now acid blue. But much more importantly, it turns out that neither of the diminutive Spaniards is in fact Spanish!

He's called Felipe and comes from Uruguay, and she's Italian and her name is Letizia. They only speak Spanish to each other because she learned it at school and he has no Italian.

"Did you have better things to do?" Uruguayan Felipe teases me in English about my non-appearance at the park. So I explain, also in English, that on Friday evening, after I'd left friend-of-a-friend Aaron, I cycled up to Prenzlauer Berg with Sven to see our chum José's collage exhibition, and that, extraordinarily, José sold a bunch of big pieces to a collector for sixteen hundred euros, which is an unparalleled victory among our crowd, and that Sven and I helped José celebrate by relaxing our rules and having seven beers each, which is also fairly unparalleled, and that it ended up with dancing and kissing and saying marvellous things to each other and so on, and that consequently we weren't up for anything at all on Saturday until the evening. As usual, my English is too rapid for Felipe and he smiles politely, none-the-wiser. At least, I think it's polite. I reckon there's something a bit superior about his manner actually. Plus his head's too large for his body.

Orange hijab woman has exchanged orange for a rather handsome British racing green, and my greater acceptance by the group is dramatically signalled when, unprompted, she instigates a conversation with me. I'd given up making any headway with her, or with any of the Arab women really; they keep so much to themselves. Nevertheless, she tells me that, while her nickname is Bonbon, her proper name is Khadra, and she confides in me – I can hardly believe it – that she's a little more than a month pregnant and she spent most of the weekend feeling sick. Then she requests that I refrain from telling anyone else. Flattered, I immediately consent. Alright, she's goofy and gauche in class, but milling together outside the school in the sunshine, I find something almost touching about her massively prominent upper gums and the fact that croissant flakes doggedly hang from her lower lip. I reckon much of her disruptive noise and lengthy unwanted arias result from a lack of worldliness. She gets easily over-excited, bless her.

Most of my classmates, I'm coming to understand, are on their second or third migration – which exposes another of my delusions – that, being the oldest, I'm necessarily the most travelled. Khadra's studied in Rome for four years, and on top of her other languages, she's picked up what she calls "a bit of English here and there", though it's really a hell of a lot of English. Not only that, but she and her husband, fellow-Tunisian Taher, run some kind of agricultural import/export business and live near Hackescher Markt. I'm left with the impression of a much more substantial person than the one I'd glibly called "orange hijab woman". Sorry sorry, *mea culpa*.

I'm a little bit jealous of Khadra because Hackescher Markt, always busy but strangely peaceful, bisected by tramlines at street level and elevated train tracks above, is one of the loveliest squares in Mitte (once you've accepted the constant threat of being mown down by the yellow, Panzer-like trams). The sudden cool darkness under the railway arches, little islands of trees and a cacophony of buildings old and new, mean that whichever way you turn, you're offered a window into yet another of Berlin's dramatic, traumatic past lives.

Back in class, there's a discussion about department stores in which Mervyn excels by reeling off "Men's, Women's, Children's, Accessories, Hats, Shoes, Handbags" in fluent German. When Almut wants to know what our largest monthly expense is, everyone replies "rent", except Mervyn who unselfconsciously replies "clothes". Some laugh; others look a bit disgusted; Joo doesn't understand. We learn about the bureaucracy involved in buying products sight-unseen (i.e. when you buy 'a cat in a sack' as the Germans would say), and the extensive customer rights which the inevitable mass of paper work confers. Karole wants us all to know that she "picks up" her clothes in New York and Singapore, and that customer service in Germany is poor. She's not happy with the attitude of Berlin's shop staff. It's true. Older Berliners who are acclimatised to Soviet ways can often seem gruff. But she's not allowed to expound on her theme because Mira interrupts. Evidently no mouthpiece for Castro's perpetual revolution, the Cuban is quick to denounce the limited choice on offer in the city's clothes stores. And we're off into another endless general chat.

Mira lacks volume control, and like Khadra, is unwilling to let her limited vocabulary inhibit her. When a thought comes into her head, she confidently opens her mouth to utter it, even when she possesses literally none of the words to do so, as if speaking German is a magic trick she hasn't yet mastered. In place of concepts or lost words, she gesticulates wildly, whistles and claps. The result is more Spanish than German, and alarmingly martial. Almut indulges her, smiling with only the tiniest hint of pity.

Since Roberto got his restaurant job, he and Francesca have bought a TV, and so we're entertained to an oration on what they saw last night – a documentary about German reunification. Like Khadra, Roberto is a master at the 'eeeeeeerm' trick. It reminds me of an actor I once worked with who was so tedious that, when he talked to you, he would tightly grip your arm to prevent your escape.

So my young Italian classmate describes every facet of this wretched documentary by providing an outline of the German unification process from the early '90s to the present with an urgency that suggests no one's ever watched TV or knows what history is. Like the rest of us, Roberto takes minutes to deliver a single sentence, and you can guarantee, after all the effort, it'll be incomplete, contradictory, irrelevant, unamusing, predictable and very short indeed. The upshot of which is that, by the end of class, we've done nothing since break but discuss shopping and TV, which feels, to put it mildly, somewhat unsatisfactory.

I leave for home in the company of Karole. She takes the opportunity to re-introduce the referendum topic. I've never managed to have a proper, uninterrupted conversation about it with her but, as we untie our bikes, she asks the inevitable question.

"Remain."

"Me too."

Oh thank God.

It's getting impossible to be pleasant to those who pledge to vote the other way, and in that regard some people turn out to be great surprises. My chiropractor in London, a man I trust with my spine, told me on my last visit that he intends to vote Leave! Obviously, I'll have to find a new chiropractor. And I've actively enjoyed unfriending Facebook friends whose Leave-supporting associates have taken to trolling me.

Karole confides that she's opting to stay in the EU for selfish reasons to do with resident status and tax, but confesses that her father is all for Leave. Given that he's a Manchester-based Botswanan Labour voter, I'm puzzled that he's happy to get into bed with people who talk about closing the borders. She assures me, he's lived so long in England that he doesn't regard himself as an immigrant.

It feels like a schism is emerging in Britain between the old, who seem to have an instinctive allegiance to Leave, and the young who are allied to Remain. I've picked it up in loads of conversations on trains and tubes whenever I've visited. "I suppose I'll go for Remain, but my dad's all for Leave." Or: "My parents are committed Leavers, but I'm thinking of voting Remain." With sixteen- and seventeen-year olds banned from voting, and students traditionally unwilling to get to the polling booths, I don't suppose those choosing Leave will be thinking about the lives of those who'll be most impacted by their decision.

Still, Karole's staunch in her father's defence. I'm sure she doesn't intend it, but by mindlessly parroting his Brexity opinions, she begins to convey the passion of the true Leaver. Of course, it's easy to be energised when you're throwing in the towel and walking away from something. Regressive, insular and in thrall to that maniac Farage, the Leavers are easily aroused to passion, while the task of remaining and reforming seems impossible to get excited about. They've got all the best lines, too. Take Back Control! Independence Day! The Remainers' strongest line is, well, Remain. I doubt they'll be the ones most motivated to get off their arses and down to the polling stations on the day.

A wave of despair washes over me as I realise it's news to Karole that Corbyn, the entire shadow cabinet and a large majority of Labour MPs intend to vote Remain. Proving little for the effectiveness of the party's contribution to the campaign, she enquires, "How are you meant to know that?" She's sure it would be news to her dad too, adding that, considering he's seventy-years-old, he has wonderful skin and hair. Really amazing it is.

Tuesday 14ᵗʰ June

Bad news and good news. While the odds are narrowing on a Leave victory, Dad's being ambulanced home in time for the Portugal/Iceland match. How brilliant is that? But still no decision has been made about our long-planned weekend trip to see them. Sven's parents, who've yet to meet my folks, have arranged to join us there so there's loads riding on it. We'll just have to wait and see how he fares over the next few days.

The first thing that happens in class is that Almut provokes me, as I knew sooner or later she would, into talking about the referendum. Specifically, she wants to know whether I think there's a chance that success lies within Herr Farage's grasp. Surely, she insists, the British people aren't stupid enough to believe what they're being told by the xenophobes.

What immediately flits through my mind is the tweet I read this morning from Graham Norton, the chat-show host: "A complicated debate obviously; but it's surely safe to say that if Farage, Johnson and Gove think something is a good idea, we can assume it isn't". Years before his TV fame, Graham played a small part in my first play, and now I think: wouldn't he make a great prime minister? God knows, he couldn't do worse than the incumbent.

But I have no time to figure out how to translate Norton to the class because the whole discussion stalls when some people don't know what Brexit is. Khadra does, but Fairuz and Leyla don't. Jang-Mi does while Woong doesn't, although, when it's explained to him, he realises he does. Joo definitely doesn't. Having outlined the basics, Almut turns to me again. In fact, all eyes are on me. There's so much I'd like to convey, but not much of it can I just 'shake out of my sleeve' as the Germans like to say.

"*Ich denke, dass...* um... *wir vielleicht wir... sind weg...* um... *Ja.*" (Which is not even close to accurate German for 'I think we're out.')

"*Nein! Aber warum, wieso?*" asks Almut – "Why?"

"*Es wird eine Katastrophe*" I offer, limply.

Almut, surprised, enquires again, "Why?"

What I would like to explain to her is that, after forty-three years of membership, it's only in the last few weeks that many of my countrymen and women have started to wonder what the Union actually is. I'd also very much like to help the rest of the class understand what perhaps a majority in the UK suppose: that the EU hasn't ever been something to take seriously; that when Winston Churchill declared that a United States of Europe should be created, he didn't mean we should be *in* it; that British culture, from high politics to low comedy, ensures that continental politics remains uncool or even a joke; and that any engagement with the ludicrous idea of a federal Europe is no better than distasteful, with ever-closer integration only serving to reinforce the fact that those silly Europeans are ridiculous, weak and probably corrupt (though we'd like to retain unencumbered access to their beaches, mountains, vineyards and food). I'd also be keen to demonstrate to everyone the noxious influence of our unhinged tabloids, austerity, little Englanders, chippiness and the opening credits to 'Dad's Army'.

But I don't have the words to say any of that so I turn to Karole for help. But she's rummaging deep in her handbag, and hasn't been listening. Almut drags the irreparably wounded conversation behind a curtain and shoots it in the head, at which point Khadra pipes up with a nasty little speech against immigrants (can't she see the irony?), and medical tourists. Thankfully, Almut smothers her before she can take flight, and we're directed to revise adjectival agreements instead.

Adjectival agreements are tricky. Not only the indefinite article but the adjective itself can alter, and once you consider the four cases, the variety of endings increases exponentially. Almut's grammatical matrix to organise all this is a thing of wonder, full of lines and circles and arrows. However, she's disinclined to move her feet as she writes, so the further across the whiteboard her grid goes, the more the lines become heavy with word endings and slope down towards the floor. When she finally arrives at the genitive case, she's run out of space entirely, at which point everything's reduced to miniscule illegible letters that tumble off the bottom of the board. I become irredeemably lost, back at school in a soul-destroying maths class.

Then – oh the horror – there's another factor that contorts adjectives even further. They can be strongly or weakly inflected by the determiner, whatever the hell that is. The adjective *hoch* (tall) when strongly inflected might variously be expressed as *hoch*, *hohe*, *hohes*, *höher*, *hohen* or *hohem*, depending. I spend the next hour baffled, defeated and cross.

When we plod round the class to be tested, my brain is mush. I'm a dumb fifty-five-year-old doing a fine impression of a retarded schoolboy, 'as dumb as a bean straw' as the Germans would say. Humiliated and head-bowed, I stare at the textbook where out-of-focus words swim about. The task is simple. I only have to guess which ending goes with the adjective *klein* (little) so that it matches the gender and the case of the chosen noun. On one side of me, I can feel Roberto willing me to the correct answer. On the other, Joo is chiselling away at her notebook binder, trying to retrieve bits of torn paper stuck in the rings. I force myself back to the exercise, command the words into focus and scan the options. *Ein kleiner. Eine kleine. Ein kleines. Einem kleinen.* (A little, a little, a little, a little.) They all seem right and they all seem wrong. After a roomy silence, Mira explodes with a shrill detonation of Cuban disgust. "*Ugghhh! Ein Kleinerrrrrrrrr!*" she screams.

Oh the shame.

And then we're out of the clouds, rising above the bumpy grey toil and turmoil of grammar, up, up, up into the infinitely expansive blue sky of culture. We're introduced to Goethe no less! The great moment has come, and we are deemed worthy. Almut proudly blu-tacks to the white board a pathetically small and smudged photocopy of a black and white photograph of a plaster bust of the man, and turns to us smiling triumphantly. No more 'I need three kilos of apples' or 'This is Roberto who comes from Sicily'. It's going to be poetry and Faust and *Sturm und Drang* from here on in. Gosh.

We learn all about Goethe's time managing the theatre in Weimar, falling in and out of love with Charlotte, the 'Sorrows of Young Werther' and Lady Hamilton. But after an hour, Irish Tracey is still pronouncing him Goo-ater. She's heard Goethe spoken correctly fifty times, but she's sticking to Goo-ater. Even when Almut corrects her, she can't hear the difference, and she goes with Goo-ater for the rest of the session.

When you live here for any length of time, you realise that many cities boast an association with the revered man. It's a bit like the Saviour's toenails. You think, surely Goethe can't have lived in quite so many places, any more than Christ probably didn't grow enough toenails for the diced up three-and-a-half feet of them floating around churches in Europe. One city that can truly claim a link to the author is Dessau, because the great man visited it seven times in twenty-one years. And Dessau's significant in other ways too. Almut informs us that Schiller also spent time there, that it was the birthplace of the philosopher Moses Mendelssohn, and as well as that, it was the home of Bauhaus, and of Buchenwald.

Clang!

It's impossible to live with a German humanities professor without knowing about Walter Benjamin, and you can't know about Benjamin without learning that he said, "There is no document of civilization that is not at the same time a document of barbarism."

Germany is living proof. As so often, a location that's famous for its links to the creation of an artistic movement, a major scientific discovery or a person of supreme creative vision, will also serve as an infamous reminder of the country's bleak past. At the end of a list that chimes brightly with the greatness of Mendelssohn, Bauhaus and Goethe is the death knell of Buchenwald, a concentration camp in which tens of thousands perished.

It's at moments like this that Almut shines brightest. Feeling a duty to refer to her country's difficult history, she does so without melodrama but also without making light of it. The same thing happened the other day when, during a mundane grammar exercise, Letizia innocently used the word 'race'. Almut immediately hit the emergency brake and calmly instructed us, after making sure she'd got our full attention, that, other than *Rassismus* (racism), Germans don't use any words connected with 'race' anymore. She explained that the concept became discredited through its misuse in the Third Reich, and if we're to integrate ourselves successfully into society, we must avoid employing it in regular conversation.

Now she introduces us to yet another corker of a German compound noun: *Vergangenheitsbewältigung* – learning to come to terms with the past, specifically the horror of it. In Germany, it's a word that needed coining. Though, with delusions of a resurgent Empire England in full swing, it strikes me that the Brits could do with a course in it.

It's tough for a foreigner with limited language skills to grasp in any meaningful way what the people here make of their country's role in the events of the last century. They often refer to it in conversations between themselves, but, understandably, don't much enjoy talking about it to anyone with an unsophisticated grasp of the language. After all, how can anyone else truly understand its complexity the way they do? Certainly, it's not possible for them to make a joke about any aspect of it – unlike the Englishman with his sad and inexhaustible fascination with the glories of World War II and his tired Hitler gags.

When it comes to life under communism, a West Berliner will

often relate a story – funny, in a gallows humour kind of way – about the visit he made to the grey world of East Berlin where "there were loads of armed police and nothing to buy". Those from the East tell different kinds of tales.

I'd known our chum Bettina for more than two years when she decided to sit down with me to relate how her family had defected forty years before. The story bore all the hallmarks of a tense sequence from a spy film, and I was transfixed as she described the secrecy with which her parents' plan was hatched. She hadn't been aware that it was happening until the moment it actually happened. The family fled at night, but separately. Bettina was stuffed into the boot of the Cuban ambassador's car with no chance to bid goodbye to her cat and her friends. Thankfully, after several hours of high tension, parents and children were miraculously re-united in the West in an early morning mist on Kurfürstendamm. But Bettina's Dad, who had been a highly regarded scientist in the East, could never find interesting work after the defection. The systems had diverged too far. The West couldn't use him, and he died disillusioned.

My German/English tandem partner Jana's story is not dissimilar. Sven met her when they were at university together shortly after the Wall fell. Like Bettina, she had come from the old East, Dresden in her case, and Sven remembers her as an optimistic young woman. These days, I see much more of her than he does, and when I report her problems and her perpetual unhappiness, he struggles to recognise the woman he knew before.

Living under communism, she resisted becoming a party member. Her ambitions were rooted in a place she couldn't even visit, but once everything was suddenly available, instant happiness seemed within her grasp. That was when Sven studied alongside her. The moment didn't last long. The West couldn't provide permanent bliss, any more than anything can. When unification occurred, it was a shock for Jana to witness its flaws. Her unrealistic expectations were bound to lead to disappointment, and the reality of the new system defeated her. Now she's stuck in a stupid job, sitting all day long on the phone, trying to squeeze money out of institutions for a cause she struggles to believe in, and she wonders whether things would have been better if they'd stayed the same. The end of communism was a boon for many Germans – but not all.

Naturally, Sven's parents, being the age they are, also have traumatic stories to tell. However, it wasn't before sharing three Christmases with them that Sven's father, Dieter, felt comfortable enough to explain to me what had happened to him during the war. With his heavily wrinkled face, shock of white hair and an extravagant moustache to match, it's hard to picture old Dieter as a young boy when he, his mother and three brothers fled on foot from Königsberg (today's Kaliningrad) in '42. Entirely dependent on the protection of those they met along the way, the fatherless family trekked five hundred miles west through war-torn countryside evading first the communists and then the fascists, before arriving, the group still miraculously intact, in Lübeck, where they thrived. The family of Gabi, Sven's mother, wasn't so lucky. Now a dance teacher, and still pretty at seventy, she tells me that, as a child living with her parents in besieged Berlin, she lost her baby sister to starvation.

The Germans I've encountered generally choose to manage the past by living decently in the present. Their survival stories, or those of their parents or grandparents, prove them the victims rather than the perpetrators of the lethal forces that were unleashed in this part of the world. And when their personal histories are recounted, there's no self-pity, only quietness and bafflement.

Given Germany's past and the work it's done on itself over the last seventy years, the current surge of far-right nationalism is especially disquieting, and throws into doubt what I always thought to be true: that it's the only country in the world to have ever properly learned from its mistakes. Having been a child refugee himself, Sven's old Dad, Dieter, can't begin to comprehend the rise of Eurosceptic, anti-immigration parties such as the *Alternative für Deutschland* (AfD) and Pegida, and the proliferation of those who firebomb mosques and refugee centres.

At the moment, the AfD's rise seems like a tsunami. It received about five per cent of votes in the last federal election, seven per cent in the European elections a year later, broke into double digits the following year, and in the Saxony-Anhalt state election this year, came second with a quarter of the ballot.

I wonder who these one-in-four are. Do I know any of them?

Wednesday 15th June

The report from Teddington is that, apart from moaning about all the pills he has to take, Dad's relieved to be back home. Tweaking the medication seems to have done the trick, and his recovery has been so remarkable that he plans to drive Mum to Hampton Hill for lunch. The fish and chip shop in 'the village' possesses a magical quality for them. They go there when there's someone to grieve for or something to celebrate. So they're off for a celebratory cod.

The newspapers contain proof that, in London, rational argument is losing the day. Lord Mandelson claims, "Brexit will make the financial crash look like a walk in the park," while the TNS poll puts Leave seven points ahead.

In Berlin, summer's changed its mind. It's cool and breezy, and class seems arid. Mervyn's away because his grandma's visiting from Estonia, so things are less gay. High maintenance though he is, his classroom contributions are often funny or weird, and he has plenty to say in the breaks, so I miss him. Not all is despondency, however. I experience a personal leap forward by figuring out the meaning of two compound nouns without help from colleagues or dictionary: *Streichholzschachtel* breaks down as 'striking wood box', hence matchbox, while *Analverkehr* translates as 'anal traffic' i.e. sodomy. See? I can do this!

When break arrives, no one wants to rush out onto to the chilly street. I find myself near the class register. Evidently I've been spelling loads of names wrong. Joo's properly spelled Xiu and Leyla's really Leila. Plus all the Spanish speakers have at least three names, except Cuban Mira who has about seven.

The need for caffeine moves me outside, and I queue in the coffee place next to Almut. Her limitations as a teacher are now clear to me. She talks way too much, as if she's forgotten that *we're* the ones who need the practice. But she's good-hearted and believes in her job. The other day she managed to use only her body to convey the meaning of both 'environment' and 'cynical'. It's extremely rare that she's reduced to using English (especially as it's not the *lingua franca* for everyone – Fairuz and correctly-spelled Leila speak not a word of it). Disturbingly, I think I have a bit of a crush on her. I take far too much notice of what she looks like. Today, I'm transfixed by her new hairdo. It's a bob in steel magnolia and suits her wonderfully. Generally, she wears pretty summer skirts which show off her discus-thrower calves. But this morning she's sporting trousers which very nicely accent her luscious curvy hips. And I positively live to hear her admit she's impressed with my language-learning. So I'm happy to talk one-to-one in the hope that an encouraging compliment might come my way.

Dream on, Timothy. As we wait to order our drinks, she wants to chat about the referendum. You get a few seconds into conversation with any German right now, and they'll ask your prediction. I talk animatedly about the video of the European map with its endlessly changing boundaries until the point when the EU is created, though immediately I realise there's no need. At the merest hint of the notion of why the old EEC came into existence, we sigh and shrug and nod in unison. We know what we're talking about. It's a generational thing. And, of course, it's a continental thing.

Brits don't associate the nation-state with fascism, as a European might have cause to do. A knock on the door at 3 a.m., the thundering rattle of tanks in the street, a memory of flight, the mysterious disappearance of a neighbour or a lethal decision about whether to collude with the enemy are not part of British communal recollection, and therefore perhaps the Brit will never comprehend the need for supranationalism in the way, for example, a German or a Frenchman does. For the English, a federated United States of Europe can easily look like one more attempt by some continental state or other to gain control over the rest.

Learning German (badly)

With absurd over-ambition, I attempt to use 'Mock the Week' to demonstrate to Almut that, for most of my countrymen, Europe's just about economics. I do my breathless best to explain that yesterday I saw the latest episode on YouTube and it had me tearing out what's left of my hair. As is the British way, the panellists mined the notion that Europe is a bore, and this with only a week to go before the referendum. They scoffed and scorned, not about Johnson and Farage, but about Europe itself. They were dismissive about the most important decision the nation has faced in generations, in order to pander, as ever, to Little England. Unsurprisingly, Almut's a bit lost and suggests I switch to English. This is her break too. So I gratefully (and fluently) appraise her of my contention that British commentators and comics perpetually reinforce the presumption that Europe is too complicated and too foreign for ordinary people to get their heads round, how the poor things mustn't be troubled by it, how, in this way, a vacuum is created in which ignorance festers – an ignorance that will eventually bite us all on the arse.

In response, my long-suffering teacher is suddenly convulsed with the idea that we should spend more class time on Brexit. "You and Karole will prepare something to present to everyone!" she exclaims. "You will be 'anti' and Karole will be 'pro', or the opposite way, and we will argue." "Yes," I reply, meaning 'no'. At which point, thank God, I'm saved from further discussion because we reach the head of the queue.

The dusty little coffee shop sells a wide range of disappointingly-worthy-looking pastries, but not one of them is gluten-free. "Are you having anything to eat?" she wonders. "No," I explain, "I have an intolerance to flour." "You have an intolerance to a lot of things," she responds pertly.

Shocked and a little hurt, I flee from Almut to alert Karole about what's in store for us. But she's busy proving her social secretary credentials to Letizia and Felipe. He hasn't seen his family in Uruguay for three years – apparently the pair have no money for flights – so rather admirably or perhaps foolishly, Karole's suggesting that her Lufthansa pilot boyfriend could use his allocation of free seats to help them out. Aha, her boyfriend's a pilot. Shopping for clothes in New York and Singapore now makes a kind of sense.

I'm happy to be waylaid by Roberto, who wonders whether Sven and I ("you and your lover," as he picturesquely puts it) would like to go for a walk with him and Francesca when we all have the time. I'm ecstatic. Roberto likes me. Mission accomplished.

Leaving for home, I find myself unlocking my bike alongside Woong who wants to tell me about a play he and Jang-Mi saw last night. It was the much fêted Hamlet at the Schaubühne. First produced in 2008, when its star Lars Eidinger was approximately the right age for the part, the show continues in repertoire, and Sven and I saw it earlier in the year. I wish I could understand Woong better, but I make out enough to tell you that he liked it with reservations. Sven and I felt the same.

In comparison to the Volksbühne's left-field radicalism, the Schaubühne does actually produce proper plays, with text and actors and everything, though all of them are directed in the way of most well-subsidised German theatre, i.e. as vehicles for politically-motivated experimentation. And I use 'experimentation' to mean its opposite, in that, in my experience, it's *de rigueur* for each German theatre director to search for answers within the same arsenal of tricks and tropes as all other German theatre directors. Thus they produce fairly interchangeable results. And the production of a play that most successfully crystallised these devices was the Schaubühne's Hamlet.

Thomas Ostermeier's production is performed on mud. Not mud you can walk on, but uneven, jagged mud apparently shipped directly from the First World War, so the actors do a lot of tottering about and falling over, and Hamlet ends up eating a fair amount of it. The show opens with 'To be or not to be' (and keeps returning to it throughout) and ends with a comedy version of the fencing match, in which the Danish prince fights Laertes armed only with a plastic spoon. One of the best moments is the death of Ophelia, which I've never seen done better. In fact I don't think I've ever seen it done at all, as it's not in the play. There's the gratuitous use of microphones, loads of beer sprayed everywhere, masses of 'Castorf slow-death-moments', men dressed as women for no reason and a huge amount of singing. The song in Hamlet that I liked best was 'Theatre' by Katja Ebstein – Germany's marvellous Eurovision Song Contest entry that came second in 1980.

> You put on your mask every night
> And you play
> As the role demands
> Theatre, theatre...

Hamlet uses it as a means to introduce the idea of the play within the play, as if Shakespeare hadn't already done that in the text. But Ostermeier cut that bit. Typically, while the English revere text as if God engraved it in stone, Germans respond to it as if the girl on reception threw it together the night before.

For someone imbued in the British theatre tradition, it was thrilling to witness a 1980s Eurovision number inserted into a major state-subsidised production of a classic play without it leading to complaints in the conservative press and questions in parliament. Imagine the outrage in Stratford if Katie Mitchell slotted a Bucks Fizz track into an RSC production. Though, having said that, 'Making Your Mind Up' would be a great replacement for 'To be or not to be'.

Many of my English theatre colleagues are jealous that I live in Berlin, regarding it as the capital of theatrical novelty. I've loved some productions, from Robert Wilson at the Berliner Ensemble to Ostermeier's renderings of Kane and Ravenhill at the Deutsches Theater. But much of the city's output is entirely wasted on me. One winter evening last year, Sven and I biked with

Bettina to a 'found space' – a disused and unheated power station – in Prenzlauer Berg. And there we witnessed a great deal of studied jigging about as a Swiss lady improvised Martha Graham moves for a couple of hours. Spread out over the vast concrete floor were a few random objects, including a stuffed unicorn and some things to make noise with. And we were invited to make the noise ourselves! You could either stand and observe (and I haven't been in love with standing in the theatre since I stood to watch 'Timon of Athens' at the Globe, and all that happened was that Timon died and I got a sore back) or you could actually contribute to the sound track, and therefore, I suppose, influence the artist's moves. At the push of a button you might trigger a not unpleasant Adele track, or a looped recording of someone counting to ten in Farsi, or the hideous noise of an electronic drill distorted through a microphone in a metal bucket. My favourite part was when I snuck off with Bettina to neck a couple of Aperol spritzers in a smoky bar down the road.

The goal of German theatre directing, at least since Brecht, is to eschew emotional engagement and catharsis. Neither Sven nor I were at all touched by the plight of any of the characters in Ostermeier's Hamlet, and this would be regarded as a good thing. For all its intelligence and freshness, the Schaubühne's production neither reveals the play as the philosophically radical piece that it is, nor shows what the members of the court are personally going through. You can't tell what it's about and you don't care. In other words, there's no heart. The legacy of Brecht, Piscator, Müller, Castorf, Schleef, and Schlingensief is not about feeling. It's about instruction and an urgent need for political change. It's the opposite of what you get in England, where directors are motivated by the twin factors of generating a sense of reassurance and not losing money.

In other words, in the UK it's lots of show and lots of biz, whereas in Germany, it's all educative and good for you. A director doesn't have to consider anything as reductive as plot, as long as the political purpose is correct. In fact, soon after moving here, I realised that, German and English theatre are two wholly separate and distinct art forms. In both countries, it's class-bound and top-down, but in Germany there's little thought for entertainment, while in England there's little thought for anything else.

A young woman we met at a party told us that she'd just graduated as a dramaturg from Berlin's most celebrated theatre school. For her first job, she was interrogated by a guy who'd been asked to direct a new production of a Verdi opera in Linz. She was up for the role of his assistant. It didn't matter that she didn't like opera because it turned out that the director didn't like it either. The discussion was entirely about how they might subvert the form.

...

With a little more than a week to go before the referendum, the FT, sensing calamity, suggests that everyone invests in German Euro-Bonds. I'm forced to wonder if we're asking the right question. Onto a bed of patriotism sprinkle a dash of prejudice and a pinch of EU-ignorance, and I fear people will mentally reformulate the referendum's question 'Should the United Kingdom remain a member of the European Union or leave the European Union?' to 'Have the last forty-three years of the UK's membership of the EU made you European-ish, or are you still British?' Worse, a theatre designer colleague tells me he understands that many are so immigration-obsessed, they take the Remain/Leave choice to stand for 'Should the foreigners be allowed to Remain, or should they be made to Leave?' If that's the case, we're well and truly screwed.

Emma fails to progress. I feel schizophrenic about it. Working on an English classic in twenty-first century Berlin is a disorienting experience and, when I think about my recent visits to the theatre here, I start to feel a little unhinged. Despite all its silliness, German theatre is admirably iconoclastic, and aside from my frustrations with it, I'm often inspired by the images it throws up. But if I think about the kind of theatres *Emma* will be playing in, I'm working for an industry mired in an excessive respect for the classics. Despite its many strengths – from its emphasis on text to its unparalleled acting craft – English theatre's sunk in aspic. As I struggle throughout the afternoon, the Schaubuhne and Volksbühne tug me in one direction, while the brief of my commissioning producer pulls me in another. I long to play irresponsible Brexiter by exploding the book and seeing where all the bits land, but I fear that I'll jettison Austen's power if I play fast and loose with her sharp period language, her delicately balanced wit and her precisely selected social settings. It feels that I'm as jammed in my paid work as I am in class – between my English Englishness and my desire to become something different – and it strikes me as wryly amusing to think that a strangely similar quandary currently faces England itself: to hunker down on its old English identity, or to open up to difference, cooperation and the future. Stumbling and indecisive, I fail to guide *Emma* along a route between the two irreconcilable extremes until five, when Jana drops in for our weekly tandem session.

She and I sit on the sunny terrace admiring Sven's green-thumbed achievements (the Germans have green thumbs not fingers) before she confides in me in English that her husband became hopelessly drunk at his birthday party at the weekend and broke some of her greatly cherished Meissen vases made in the East and inherited from her grandmother. Lilly has become uncommunicative, Lukas has got into trouble by chaining himself to the school railings in a provocation against climate change and Jana herself has made absolutely no effort to investigate how to realise her dream of teaching cookery to kids.

Switching languages, we discuss hooliganism at the European Football Championships (the Russians and the English are behaving like Nazis), and Bob Geldof. There have been revolting scenes from the River Thames where he and Farage lead rival flotillas, trading insults and looking like twats. Yes, Geldof's correct to highlight the fact that Farage, an MEP and member of the EP's Fisheries Committee, has attended only one of its forty-three meetings. But the incident – a kind of regatta with rich blokes bawling through megaphones at each other – makes both sides look repellent. Showbiz for ugly people. Surely the stakes are too high for this kind of shit.

Thursday 16th June

It began ten days ago – the certainty that I was going to prosper as never before with a new class and my shiny new textbook. Unsullied, its pages silky and chemically fresh, it smelled of the Munich factory in which it was printed, and it promised nothing but a fast track to fluency. I hardly dared look directly at it, with its linguistic hieroglyphs and grammatical ciphers beyond my comprehension. Simply having it on the desk in front of me produced a thrilling shudder of anticipation.

Then reality hit. Mired once again in blasted adjectival endings, yet again it's a disaster. Trying to cheer me, Karole whispers that as long as we mumble, no one'll notice whether our adjectives agree or not, but I'm too depressed to laugh it off.

If only I could spend the hours after class revising what we study in the morning, I might do better. But I run home to grapple with the language of 19th century England. If after that, when Sven returns from work, he'd chat to me in German, that would also help a lot, but when six o'clock comes round, we both need to relax, so we spend the evening in English. I might be aided a bit if his friends weren't so eager to use me to practise their language skills. But whenever they see me, it's not with a sense of duty that they seize the chance to improve their English – they actively love it and can't wait to get started. They adore speaking anything that's not German. It's a national fetish. For whatever reason (and it's almost certainly political-historical), modern Germans are massively drawn to the non-native. While the English want things to be nice and homely, the German takes pleasure in things being foreign. And even if I try to deny them the opportunity to speak English with me, they won't stick to German pure and simple. They stuff their speech with alien words and witty references to third-party cultures. To a Brit, behaviour of this kind in English would at best be unseemly, and at worst the result of a treacherous soul.

Learning German (badly)

But to a German, it's proof of a good education and an open mind, and nothing to be ashamed of.

But it's not just *Emma* and Sven and his friends who are the problem. I've yet to be served by anyone in Weinmeisterstraße's Urban Outfitters who can speak German. Waiters in some restaurants in Kreuzberg can only speak English. Everyone at the gym does. Even the ladies behind the sausage and cheese counter in my local supermarket are willing to have a go. Honestly in the last two weeks, outside of Wassertorstraße and my sessions with Bettina and Jana, I've not said anything more complex than 'hello', 'goodbye', and 'I'd like two hundred grams of mince.'

So why on earth am I bothering?

Because I must, given the ever-narrowing odds on Brexit. Because I'm excited about the time I'll be able to read books and plays in the original language. Because Charlemagne believed that 'to learn another language is to possess a second soul'. And because, to be honest, I'd be content if I could just get a bit more out of Christmas with Sven's family. Though they have a decent level of English, they're much more comfortable in German, and I'd like to be more comfortable with them.

Plus, aren't I being desperately rude if I live in a foreign city and expect everyone I encounter to speak English just for me? So on I struggle, not working at it very hard, behaving towards the whole studying lark as if I'm a tourist, as if this isn't my new home, but only a temporary base.

On the other hand, I take classroom dynamics way too seriously. Good Lord, it wasn't so long ago that I was regularly standing up to manipulative West End divas, and holding my ground against sharky Broadway producers. Now I've fallen into the trap of behaving like a bashful, oversensitive teenager in a classroom I've allowed to become my universe. Instead of conquering adjectival endings, I judge Almut, ponder my place in the pecking order and wonder who likes me. I'm competitive for a few minutes, then fantasize about dropping out. I sulk when I'm tired or bored, eagerly join in with the power games of student vs. teacher, avoid looking clever or stupid, and refuse to expose my feelings or show vulnerability. Sheep-like, I won't rock the boat by complaining about Almut's teaching methods (we've never started on time or taken a break that hasn't overrun). All I do is moan internally.

Simply put, I love being in a classroom but resent every single thing about studying. It's tragic.

And I'm no better nor worse than my fellows. We are, none of us, prodigies. People are often absent for vast stretches of time – I don't think Bled from Albania has shown up more than twice – and, with the possible exception of a sweet bespectacled Ukrainian called Milica who's way ahead of the pack, nobody ever gets anything much right. Not more than one in twenty of my attempts to pronounce *ch* goes well, and at the end of a word, I can't tell an 'e' from an 'a'. My close rustly neighbour Xiu rarely bothers with the ends of words at all. Her version of *haben* (to have) is *habe*. "*Haben*!" Almut cheerily prompts. "Remember the endings!" Seconds later, Xiu pronounces *Guten Morgen* as *Gute Mon* and Almut lets it go. In Karole's mouth, *schön* is 'shring'. Tracey thinks *wird* is 'vish'. When Melina attempts 'eighty-eight' (*achtundachtzig*), it comes out more like "*Achtung! Achtung!*" and Almut just laughs. *Sie* is a word that Jang-Mi must have been taught on day one of the A-1-1 module. It means 'she', 'they' and 'you', and is pronounced 'zee'. But each time she meets it, she offers a different reading, presently favouring 'sigh'.

Occasionally, our investigation throw up something fun. The word *Zeug* tickles me. It means 'thingy' or 'stuff' – 'stuff you need for stuff'. So *Schwimmzeug* is 'stuff for swimming', i.e. a swimming costume. *Spielzeug* is 'stuff for playing', i.e. a toy. Best of all, *Flugzeug* is 'stuff for flying', i.e. an aeroplane!

Sometimes, when we get things wrong, we're hilarious. For instance, 'half past one', or 'half one' as we say in English, is translated as 'half two' in German. Brits look backwards, Germans look forwards – highly appropriate given current events. Having mastered time, Almut moves us on to study how to measure the length of things, and for 9.5 meters, I suggest 'nine metre fifty' (*neun Meter fünfig*), which turns out to be correct. Karole guesses 'nine-one-half meter' (*neuneinhalb Meter*), which sounds weird but is also correct. Remembering how to tell the time, Melina goes for 'half ten meters'. Wrong but adorable.

My favourite funny German word at the moment is *Ufer*. It means riverbank and it always makes me chuckle. OO-FAH! Another perennial favourite is *Ausfahrt* (exit) because of the fart bit at the end. By break time, I'm giggling with Karole over the past tense of *essen* (to eat), which in the first person, is *aß*, pronounced 'arse'. Forgive me – it was hot and we were hungry.

Nonsense aside, the real disaster is that, while I'm making ridiculously slow headway in German, I'm losing English faster than a cat sheds hair in spring. The other day, when I wanted to say 'ground almonds', I could remember neither 'ground' nor 'almonds'. Desperate to stem the flow, I've taken to writing down things I can't remember – by which I mean I write them down later when I recall them, obviously! – and a glance at the list tells me that, in the last forty-eight hours, I've failed to come up with disc, slipstream, lugubrious and Sarkozy. Plus I said marzipan when I meant parmesan. Perhaps it's just old age. As Jeremy Hardy would say, 'You know, this was all fields when I was a girl.'

After the break, Almut partially remembers yesterday's coffee shop conversation, and invites me to address the class in defence of the Remain campaign. I glance at Karole for help, though once again, she's unavailable – this time engrossed in a nail emergency.

Remembering my last tragic attempt to explain Brexit to my fellow students, I decide to keep it light by describing an amusing post I saw this morning. I'm pretty confident I've got the words for it, and, though it's simple and comic, I believe it seriously nails why the EU is a good thing and why we should therefore Remain.

History of Europe:

War
War
War
War
War
War
War
Arguments about bananas.

To be honest, I'll probably go with
banana arguments. #remain

As I begin to unpack it, I sense no one understands what the hell I'm talking about. People are aware that it's a serious subject, so why am I trying to be funny? The Koreans look anxious. Why am I making light of war? The Arabs are confounded. Why am I nattering about 'nanas? Karole cocks an eyebrow. It's a terrible, horrible, ignominious failure. I can neither communicate my passion for things European nor make anyone laugh. I am nothing. I am no one.

So thank Christ for Tracey. At least she makes me feel a bit better about myself. Poor thing, she still hasn't even understood the idea that English is *verboten* in class. When Almut sets us homework about writing dialogue featuring two friends talking about a third, Tracey doesn't understand the word for dialogue. It's *Dialog*, pronounced something like 'dee-a-loag'. "What? Write what now?" she asks, panicking and doggedly sticking to her first language. "*Dialog*," Almut repeats. "What?!" repeats Tracey, shaken. "*Dialog*," Almut tries again, and even translates it into English for her: "Dialogue." "Oh, dialogue!" echoes Tracey, relieved. "I heard earlobe."

When things go badly in class, I envisage a future in which

Learning German (badly)

I'll never be able to communicate with my classmates, or – much more calamitously – one in which I'll forever be a fake German-Englishman, imprisoned in his own language, isolated and unreachable. At such times, it becomes vitally important that things go well with work so that I can at least feel compensated by the knowledge that I'm still able to communicate with an English audience who understands me. And, today, after weeks of torment with *Emma*, I make the breakthrough I've craved.

This is my solution: Emma Woodhouse will be the embodiment of England in Brexit times. Like England, she believes herself to be uniquely clever, but, just like her country, she's her own worst enemy. She wishes never to marry but to organise everyone else's marriages. Likewise, England wishes to go it alone in the belief that it can rule the world as it did before. Hubristically, Emma thinks she can be rude to her neighbours and they won't notice because they're not important. Ditto England. Her father, crusty valetudinarian Mr Woodhouse, will be a cross between Gove and Johnson, living in the past, superficially charming but effortlessly manipulative. Mr Churchill is Farage, the scheming, amoral cad. Harriet Smith will be cast as Ireland. Apparently powerless, in the end she proves to be the person who brings Emma to her knees. Mrs Elton is the Tory party, grand and oblivious, and Miss Bates the voting British public, burdened by austerity and cruelly misinformed. At the dénouement, Emma (England) discovers the truth about the devious actions of Mr Churchill (Farage), rejects him and embraces the goodness of Jane Fairfax (who, with her meek intelligence, plays the soul of England's better future). Realising her flaws, Emma finally deserves to fall in love with Mr Knightley (Chuka Umunna?), which brings about the longed-for happy ending. Her maturation admits her into the larger society, while England votes to Remain, elects to live in harmony with its neighbours and all is well. I think it's inspired. I've managed to synthesise the old and the new, by being faithful to me – both the lover of the English classic, and the new expressionistic German me. I feel relieved and exhausted, which is always a good sign. However, I decide not to phone my commissioning producer straight away. I've learned to let ideas settle overnight before announcing them to the world. Content with hard work well done, I look for a little relaxation online.

Checking my phone, I come face to face with news that a Labour MP called Jo Cox has been stabbed and shot by some kind of white supremacist in a small town in Yorkshire. All the newspapers and all my feeds are buzzing with it. Reports indicate he shouted "Britain first" and "Death to Traitors" as he wielded the knife.

I've never heard of Cox but from what I read, it sounds like she was a totally decent person, and a politician determined to make the world a better place. It's hard to imagine how this'll affect the referendum. It's pretty bloody galling to listen to racist UKIP Leavers express condolences.

My optimism about Emma and her victory over the Leave campaign suddenly feels horribly misguided and premature.

...

While Sven stays in to watch the Germany/Poland match in the Euros, I cycle over to Bettina's to look at another poem. This time she's chosen *Todesfuge* (Fugue of Death) by Paul Celan, which begins...

> *Schwarze Milch der Frühe wir trinken*
> *sie abends*
> *wir trinken sie mittags und morgens*
> *wir trinken sie nachts*

> Black milk of daybreak we drink it
> at evening
> we drink it at midday and morning
> we drink it at night

Learning German (badly)

...and which goes on to evoke life lived in a Nazi death camp, which was where the poet's parents died, and from where he himself managed to escape before working for the Red Army, after which he studied in the east, escaped to the west and committed suicide in 1970.

Bettina patiently takes me through the work, revealing its meaning both in terms of the words, and also what's below, above and wrapped around them. Minka moves in and negotiates a place on her mistress' lap. With her insistence on nothing but human touch, she demonstrates her disregard for our morbid subject.

Wine is poured, and we relax. Bettina says she's spent the last few weeks exploring her father's letters. He died earlier in the year and she's full of discoveries. Apparently, we've reached that level in our friendship when she feels able to confide in me the history of her family's war. Still reeling from the news about Jo Cox, I'm in the mood for something cathartic.

Of all the details Bettina gives me about her father, I'm particularly struck by the fact that, having found himself in a labour camp in the USSR at war's end, it wasn't until 1947 that he was finally sent back home to Germany. During his lifetime, he never spoke to anyone about the impact his experiences in Russia had on him, and only now is Bettina learning the truth.

She shows me some of the letters he penned during his career as a soldier, prior to capture by the Soviets. In several sent to a pen-pal on *Wehrmacht* letter-headed paper, he refers to anti-Semitism and openly remarks that he thinks it no better than shit.

At the same time, Bettina's Mum was a sixteen-year-old living in Chemnitz. Bettina says she'd been anti-Nazi from a young age – not for any high-minded reason, but simply because she was anti-everything. One day, as a child taken to watch the Führer parade through town, she was hoiked onto her father's shoulders to get a good view. On returning home, her mother enquired whether she'd given the customary *Hitlergruß* (the infamous salute), but she dismissed the idea with a scornful, "I'm not mad".

Without regarding her parents as heroic, Bettina's proud of the fact that, at least in private, they were opposed to the genocidal regime.

On the other hand, as a girl, her aunt thought the whole thing was terrific because it involved bags of community activity and organised fun. Bettina's grandmother was equally supportive of Nazism – in her case because trade flourished under Hitler and as a shopkeeper, she did well. As the family's breadwinner, Grandma was obliged to earn. Her husband, Bettina's grandfather, had been injured in the First World War and could only perform trivial, badly paid jobs. Since 1917 he'd lived with a permanent headache, and when the Second World War was declared, he was given a low-level administrative task in a concentration camp. It wasn't hard for him to figure out what was going on, and before the war's end, he killed himself.

All this time, Minka has been purring on Bettina's leg, the happiest of cats.

Friday 17th June

Great news is that Dad's decided that he's feeling well enough to cope with guests, so our weekend trip is on. Arrangements have been slimmed down a bit, and we're going to spend less time with them than originally planned. Still, we're all definitely convening in Teddington at my parents' home tomorrow, and Mum's started cooking. As arranged with Almut, I'm leaving class during break in order to make the tea-time flight to London with Sven.

More good news is that Mervyn's back. He reports rather touchingly that his grandma's stay was so fabulous, three days felt like one. Apparently, she brought two suitcases with her, one of which was entirely filled with food: bread, vodka, sour cream, meat and fish. Fish in a suitcase? Absolutely! Mervyn lists the types and their functions: eel for lunch, herring for dinner, dry fish for picnics, codfish for any time, fish that's good for fish & chips, and fish you're only meant to eat in a cinema. Who knew?

There's been no further mention of the walk Roberto suggested, but I guess we've all been busy. At the weekend, while I was scoffing strawberries in the sunshine and seeking out contemporary art in challenging buildings, he spent thirty-six hours indoors at a rave in Neukölln drinking, smoking and listening to heavy metal bands I've never heard of. In Palermo, as a fifteen-year-old, he tells me that his day would start in a bar, where he'd neck a litre-and-a-half of wine before progressing to the park with a bottle of pastis. Unfortunately, though perhaps not unsurprisingly, he's developed a stomach problem and has had to give up alcohol entirely. "And coffee," he adds, sheepishly looking down at the espresso in his hand. He's sneezing and snorting "like a whole herd of bison", as Noel Coward would say, rearranging the contents of his nasal passages to create an aural landscape one normally associates with heavy furniture being dragged around. I look for ways of escape, but Almut's already started the class.

With weaponised charm, I offer him a tissue and gently point out the sizeable scrap of cigarette paper stuck in his hair.

We begin with one of our teacher's great speeches on Ramadan, by which she showcases her knowledge of all things Islamic and dollies up to the Arab ladies.

I'm disappointed I've made so little headway with them, Khadra aside. If, by chance, our eyes should meet, Leila looks terrified. And Fairuz, whenever she bothers to turn up, continues to resist any social attempt I make. She slouches in and out of school like a surly sack of potatoes, chewing cardamom seeds and behaving as if the whole thing's nothing more than a break from housework. She's got four kids and has lived in Berlin for fifteen years (Karole told me), but you wouldn't know it because her German's worse than mine. Whenever a new concept's introduced, her normal response is to laugh. You don't have to be an intellectual to learn a language (obviously), but a little more mental engagement wouldn't do any harm. Fairuz's biggest crime, in my view, is that she never EVER remembers to put the verb in the second position, despite the fact that putting the verb in the second position of a sentence is the number one rule in German, and is such a basic thing to know that I believe she should be instantly demoted from A-2-2 back down to A-1-1, if not expelled. Instead, she is humoured.

In response to Almut's address on Ramadan, Fairuz and Leila perform tight-lipped smiles and look down at their books. Are they humbled by the fact that a non-Arab person is passionately engaged in their situation, or would they simply prefer not to be reminded that there's a long time to wait until dinner?

In terms of cultural relativism, it's fair to say that Cuban Mira's a girl with 'tomatoes over her eyes', as the Germans say, and on cue, she declares impassioned hostility to the whole notion of Ramadan, demanding to know why Leila insists on starving her daughter between sunrise and sunset. At least she's practising her German, I suppose. But who wants to take up the challenge of a rebuttal? Khadra's absent, Fairuz pretends not to have heard, and Leila has no interest in arguing. Nevertheless, from beneath black hijabs, dark eyes blaze with eloquence. 'Mira's an idiot,' they contend.

Then Almut turns to me. Almost as exercised about Brexit as she is about Ramadan, she's curious to know what the Brits think of the recent twist in the sorry saga – Jo Cox's murder and the simultaneous launch of Farage's latest effort, 'Breaking Point', a poster featuring a long, dense queue of Middle-Eastern people. Both were reported heavily on German news channels last night. Farage's slogan reads, "We must break free from the EU and take control of our borders". But it implies: Vote Leave or get overrun by brown people. As he faced the cameras, Farage's expression was part anxious/part smug, and slack-jawed disbelief that he was getting away with it.

A descendant of Huguenot refugees who's married to a German, he's like an on-line ad you can't click away. Having failed to get elected to the House of Commons seven times, he nevertheless pops up over and over to speak for us all on immigration. Still, I suppose the image – a year-old photo of a crowd of exhausted Syrian refugees trudging along a road towards Slovenia – will pack a punch with those who distrust facts, and fear people with whom they can't immediately identify. In the face of such ugly emotional manipulation, is there any purpose in pointing out that Syrian asylum seekers have nothing to do with the free movement of EU citizens, that none of the people featured on the poster have subsequently come to Britain, and that, in any case, Germany's doing fine having accepted a million of them?

"Farage didn't kill Jo Cox, but..." I falter, faced with a thought that contains several words I don't know. Thankfully, Almut can sense my determination, and encourages me patiently. Even so, the best I can do is something that roughly translates as, "But if you say people must be angry, people get angry." In my head, it sounded so much more eloquent, something to do with the fact that when you encourage rage, you shouldn't be surprised when people become rageful. If you present politics as a matter of life and death, like Farage does, is it really a shock when someone takes you at your word and kills those who hold different views? At least I've said something, and Almut has helped, and people have listened, and maybe understood.

We then move on to a Q&A about telephones. Karole is asked: When was the telephone invented? 1567 or 1877?

"Umm..." she prevaricates, unsure.

I'm forced to change my mind about Karole on a daily basis. Serially, I've considered her fun, fake, admirable and beautiful. On different days, I've thought she was irksome and I've liked her loads. Today, I wonder whether she's simply thick. And the awful thing is that she's the only Brit I see regularly. I've never before missed having English mates to talk to, but with the situation deteriorating fast back home, I do now.

On the subject of phones, we discuss the mobile, i.e. what the Germans call the *Handy*. If *Public Viewing* (by which they mean watching sport communally) is my favourite wrongly re-attributed German word, *Handy* is my second. One *Handy*, two *Handys*. Another fine example is *Mobbing*. The English might mob pop stars, but in Germany it's children who get mobbed, because they use *Mobbing* to mean bullying. An *Evergreen* is an old song. An *Oldtimer* is not a person but a vintage car. A *Dressman* is a male model who might wear a *Smoking* (a dinner jacket) or even a *Pull-under* (a tank top). You don't ride a *Pony* – it's a fringe. A *Messie* is a hoarder, and, if you're a *Tramper,* you hitchhike. A *Shooting Star* is an overnight success and a *Joker* is a footballer who comes on late and scores goals, what my dad calls a 'super sub'.

Sticking to phones, everyone seems shocked to learn that, under communism, it was only the politically well-connected East Berliner who could own a phone. The majority of my classmates live on or near the border between the old East and West, but it's clear to Almut that they know next to nothing about life pre-'89. So we receive a rambling lecture that might be called 'Then and Now', in which Almut catalogues some of the impact of the Cold War on Berlin, beginning with the effect the Wall had on its dialects and accents, and ending with a description of the *Geisterbahnhöfe*, the inner city 'ghost stations' that straddled the two halves of the divided city, between which free movement was severed, and around which, protected by barbed wire, heavily armed guards patrolled night and day.

The *Tränenpalast* (Palace of Tears) stands next to the train station on Friedrichstraße, just as it did before the Wall fell. Then it was the old East Berlin processing hall for those with a visa to transit west through the station. Now it's a museum where the grim reality of the location as a *Grenzübergang* (border crossing) is on show, with a vivid recreation of the way in which citizens' desires were thwarted by the pitiless intransigence of a militarised bureaucracy. I wonder how many of my classmates can envisage the station as it was then, being so familiar with it as it is now: a permanently crowded, non-descript spot, utterly free of tears, where you can pop in for a McDonald's or a greasy kebab on your way home from a club.

On the subject of accents, Almust tells us that there was great pride to be had under communism in being a working-class East Berliner and sounding like it, while capitalist West Berlin aspired upwards and thought of itself as more refined. The western half was isolated and poor, lacking industry and infrastructure. Young people deserted the place for jobs elsewhere, while students from every other part of Germany flooded in to take advantage of subsidies and tax cuts. The result was that their voices overwhelmed and diluted the indigenous accent, which simultaneously thrived in the East. If you know what to listen for, you can still hear the difference.

Sven has described to me how the German language, to an extent, became two languages, the west integrating a slew of American words, whereas the east embraced Soviet terms, at least officially. Astronaut vs. *Kosmonaut* is the often cited example. Small things can cause controversy in conversations between *Ossis* and *Wessis* even now. Don't get them started on how to say 'plastic bag'. You'll be waylaid for hours listening to an argument about the virtues and vices of *Plastiktüte* (west) and *Plastetüte* (east).

Even seventy years after the war and more than a quarter century after the Wall, Berlin still displays its battle scars. Amid the abandoned communist monuments and restored palaces, entirely renovated streets and painstakingly reconstructed churches, lie patches of empty nothingness – evidence that the old East lacked the funds to finish the job properly. Look closely at some of the restoration, and you can easily see that it was done fast and on the cheap. The *Nikolaiviertel*, Berlin's historic heart, is characterised by streets lined with obviously fake eighteenth-century mansions that wouldn't be out of place in Disneyland. Considering its post-war starting point, the rebuilding of the city is nevertheless something of a miracle. In 1945, some inhabitants were boiling wallpaper and eating the paste residue in order to survive. The currency was worthless and people bartered for everything. Today, with its inner city leafiness and imperial monuments, Berlin feels like a cross between Vienna, Moscow and Milton Keynes. Grand palaces sit adjacent to concrete communist follies that border sublime shaded parks where memorials to atrocities and catastrophes nestle among the trees. House building never stops and inward migration continues to rise, but the spiritual centre of one of the world's most functional social democracies definitely feels under-populated.

Saturday 18th June

The parental conclave is convened in Teddington, one of London's more verdant suburbs. Not only have the two couples never met before, but England is entirely new to Gabi and Dieter, who've made the journey not only to be introduced to my parents, but also to enjoy Sunday with some old friends who relocated from Bremen to Brighton last year. Before Dad's recent hospital stay, Sven and I had planned to spend the entire weekend with my parents, but one day of entertaining is enough for them right now, so we're going to have a night in London instead. Sven and I will rendezvous with Gabi and Dieter tomorrow evening in Gatwick, from where we'll return to Germany and march together through the "arrivals from the EU" customs portal. Will I still be eligible this time next year, I wonder?

I'm shocked to see how much frailer Dad looks, though typically he's determined to play down his recent setback, and behaves as if it never happened. My only misgiving about how smooth the event might go springs from childhood memories of him declaring, "The only good German's a dead German!" whenever the country or its inhabitants were mentioned.

Like me, both Mum and Dad are from London's south suburbs. Dad's parents chose not to evacuate him during the bombing. So, while Mum was sent to live with a bunch of kind strangers in North Derbyshire, he would go to the top of Sydenham Hill to watch the capital's buildings burn and the flames turn the sky blood red. Scarred by losing friends and neighbours to the 'doodlebug' and the V-2, the truth is that he's struggled to come to terms with the fact that his son's hitched his wagon to a Kraut.

And though she wouldn't say so in front of Sven, Mum's dead set against me applying for German citizenship, and she's demonstrated this reluctance by refusing to get Gabi and Dieter's names straight. Sometimes she's referred to them as Abbie and Dieter and sometimes as Gabi and Peter, but, until today, she's never got both right at the same time.

But these old folk are social pros. Joshing each other about the progress of their national football teams keeps the conversation air-bound for the first ten minutes. Still, after the initial greetings, small cultural variations reveal themselves. The Germans remove their shoes and wait patiently for *Hausschuhe*. These are terribly important things. Germans hold any number of spare ones in case a bunch of guests arrive unprepared. They have a vast variety of words for them, and most are very sweet: *Schluppen, Schluffen, Puschen, Patschen, Bambuschen* and *Pantoffeln* to name but a few. However, in Teddington, no guest slippers materialise. So, as unobtrusively as possible, Gabi and Dieter slip their outside shoes back on again. Additionally, the lack of any kind of formality before meals – in terms of toasts or official invitations to begin eating – unnerves them. When my parents start tucking in as soon as the plates are on the table, Gabi and Dieter stare open-mouthed in disbelief. But generally the event passes off swimmingly, its success due in no small measure to Mum's ability to dish up three-and-a-half meals during a four-and-a-half hour visit.

Photographs are taken of two pairs of dead ringers enjoying the easy comfort of the pale green Parker Knolls in the front room, Gabi sporting the mandatory German small-town lady's hairdo (short and no-nonsense), while my mother is typically Middlesex-bouffed. While Dad's a walking advertisement for the comfortable stylings of M&S, Dieter looks a touch more rakish with his marvellous silver moustache. Both fathers are coordinated in blue, beige and grey, and both mothers in blue, pink and purple.

When it comes to seeing them off at the railway station, my old dad has a tear in his eye. Ever since I went into the theatre, he's been terrified of who I'd end up with, but I think he's happy that his son has made a good match at last, and perhaps he even feels that he's now reached a proper rapprochement with the old enemy. Plus, of course, no doubt it's on his mind – it's certainly on mine – that there's a chance this could be the first and last such meeting.

Monday 20th June

On Prinzenstraße, Karole spots me ahead of her and careens with her bike into mine for a laugh. "Aha!," I nod, trying to find it amusing, "I haven't seen you along here. I didn't know you come to school this way." "Oh, I always find a different route," she explains, very much in Sally Bowles mode, "I can't bear to see the same boring old roads every day."

As we tie up together, she invites Sven and me to a get-together this evening in her apartment. "Yannis was meant to be flying, but now he isn't, and I feel like having people over. Just a few classmates. Last minute idea. Very casual. Come if you can." Well, how thrilling is that?!

We study questions that use the pronouns *wo, wohin* and *woher* (where, where and where), and, in order to practise, we turn to the subject of driving. Maria needs a car. No, not one of our Marias, but Maria Torremolinos, a character who inhabits A-2-2's textbook and corresponding audio CD. A young South American *au pair*, she lives in Munich with a German family and is always getting into scrapes. The greatest trouble was when she had to dispose of the trash. In the courtyard of her apartment building, she was clueless about which bin was meant for what type of rubbish, and she made the fatal error of guessing! Imagine how the caretaker shouted at her!

Separating trash is the closest thing Germany has to a state religion. In fact, the country is pretty zealous about conserving resources in general, at least *Wessis* are. Growing up with the Green revolution in the west, Sven's least favourite sound is needlessly running water. Conversely, in the east, despite an excellent recycling policy, the communists cast themselves as the masters of nature and freely provided all citizens with hot water and heating, so the *Ossi* never had energy bills to pay. Therefore, conserving wasn't a priority, and consequently old *Ossis* find it more of a wrench adjusting to the new ecologically-aware order. All the ones I know have the heating on full blast all winter, whether they're in or out.

At the conclusion of each of Maria's A-2-2 adventures, there's a whimsical reveal as the scales fall from her eyes and she sees how ridiculous her hilarious South American ways are. At which point on the CD, the actress playing Maria is required to laugh at herself at length. Generally, she begins valiantly enough, then she proceeds with less conviction, and finally she has no conviction at all. I imagine her thinking, "Not to worry, they'll fade me out. They won't want this much bad laughing-acting." But they don't fade her out. Not for ages and ages. It's excruciating.

In the afternoon, I visit Jana and sit with her on her spacious balcony among her carefully arranged cacti. For most of our forty English minutes, I berate my tandem partner about solid leftie Labour MPs Gisela Stuart and Kate Hoey and the mystery of how they could campaign alongside Brexit freaks Carswell and Cummings, especially Stuart. "I mean, she's German! Why doesn't she know better?" Switching to Jana's language, she tells me that, miracle of miracles, her husband's sought help for his drinking. He visited a hypnotherapist, and for two days things looked up, until the weekend came round and he forgot that champagne contained alcohol. After knocking back *Sekt* and hurting his arm slipping on the stairs, there followed twenty-four hours of shame and self-flagellation and a declaration that it would never happen again.

But all is not lost. Jana shyly lets me know that, during one of his two sober days, she felt motivated to visit a kid's cookery school on the other side of town. She quizzed the woman who runs it, and is now armed with at least a bit of practical information about setting up her own place. We celebrate by popping round the corner to the best cake shop in the district, with a ban on correcting each other's grammatical errors until we've eaten some *Kalter Hund*. Translated as 'cold dog', no one knows why the exquisite no-bake chocolatey treat bears that name. Nevertheless, it's one of the best things about living in Germany.

Full of sugar on my bike-ride home, I have an epiphany. I allow myself for a moment to drop my burden. I think, no, surely, it's not going to happen. It can't happen. We're always being told how the electorate has an instinctive intelligence, that it doesn't get thing wrong. And once I'm back in the apartment, I glance at my phone to read that my optimism is vindicated. With three days to go, YouGov puts Remain marginally ahead. There. You see? Everything's going to be ok. And, if it isn't ok, I'll cope. I transferred shows to Broadway in my twenties. I built a theatre company in my thirties. I learned how to write plays in my forties. For goodness sake, Brexit is not going to defeat me in my fifties. At worst, what is it? Some paper work and an interview down at the town hall.

When Sven returns from work, he hasn't taken the bag off his shoulder before he throws himself into a tirade against our Libyan neighbours for never remembering to properly close the street door to the building, and for having put up an ISIS flag in one of their windows. It's not an ISIS flag, I tell him. It's a Libyan flag, and it's a massive improvement on their wretched brown rugs, but the way he's going on about it, you'd think it presages nought but evil.

He's also had a chat to the Polynesian tattoo artist, who lives next door under the brothel, and who's convinced that associates of the Libyans are living in our cellar, which, he supposes, is why they always keep the front door ajar. I remind Sven that our Polynesian friend has only just been released from a year's stretch in prison and might not be the most reliable source of intel. In fact, of what we ourselves have seen and know for certain, the Libyans' only crimes involve leaving shoes in the stairwell, dumping some old furniture in the courtyard and lighting an open flame (once) in the cellar. None of those heinous offenses has been repeated since the third floor neighbour bollocked them about it last week. Sven's a fan of lurid TV police procedurals, and I worry whether his exposure to a constant stream of televised murder, sex crimes and brown-faced terrorism is affecting his judgement. Give them time, I urge. They don't know our ways. They just need educating.

...

I'm glad that he agrees to come with me to Karole's tonight because I want him to meet my classmates and tell me what he thinks of them, and knowing our hostess and her talent for social organisation, 'the bear will be tap-dancing there'.

A summer storm is rocking the neighbourhood so we take a taxi. Berlin's taxis are not the black boxes they are in London, the sort that rigidly divide driver and passenger. They look like real cars outside and in, so you're more aware of the actual chap you've hired. Perhaps that's why Sven's developed some rules about taxi conduct, one of which forbids the holding of hands. Not that we're in the habit of holding hands at all times, but it seems to me that his is a silly rule, so I always forget about it and whenever I want his hand, wherever we are, I seek it out. As the car sets off for Karole's, I reach out, and he sharply pulls away. Instinctively, I clock the driver and notice that he's Turkish. Most Berlin taxi-drivers are.

After we've arrived at our destination, we discuss the incident because I'm hurt and he's cross, rehearsing the familiar arguments that divide "They've got to learn our ways" from "We have to respect theirs". And as with all quarrels that pivot around the gay/Muslim divide, the row is inflamed with an additional pair of oppositions that pit "There's no need to ram it down their throats!" against "I'm fifty-five years old and I'm not going to pretend not to be gay for anyone!" In the end, as is always the case when the subject comes up, we agree that the issue is unresolvable, and a bit grumpily we ring Karole's bell.

Karole and Yannis (Munich-born with Greek parents) live in one of those new, expensive-looking blocks in Mitte. They're so uniformly character-free that, gazing at them, a sliver of your soul breaks free and bursts like a soap bubble. Outside, we could be in any city in the world, but inside, Karole's decorative choices reflect her resumé. There's evidence of her African roots, her high-earning years in the States and many of her romantic affairs. In America, she explains, as she takes us on a tour of the flat, she would fill her lovers' apartments with interesting things, lose the men and keep the things. She mentions getting pregnant, once to me and also separately to Sven. Whenever she sees a baby these days, she's overwhelmed by a need to smell it, she says. But Yannis doesn't want to have kids. Additionally, he's disinclined to marry, and without a ring on her finger, she's reluctant, as she puts it, to "fall pregnant".

She's invited Roberto, but he's too sick with that thundering head cold to come. Felipe and Letizia said they'd show up. In fact, they'd promised to arrive early and "teach Karole vegan cooking", but at the last minute they bailed by text. Milica, the class swot, has turned up, playing the meek wife to colourless husband, Ostap. Ostap has a good job, he tells me ploddingly, with a reasonable income. And next year they might go on holiday to Majorca. "Soon we will buy an espresso machine," he announces with a pinch of *éclat*, turning to Milica with instructions: "You must research espresso machines." She smiles up at him with un-ironic pleasure.

Mervyn, heavily made-up and wearing a see-through shirt that accentuates his chubbiness, bounds in from the balcony with news that the storm is over and the sun has unexpectedly broken through the clouds. "I can't stay out there!" he declares, "I'll melt!"

And there's Khadra. Karole has persuaded her to come. How admirable is Karole? In my mind she is now heroic as well as glamorous. The Tunisian woman hasn't been in class for ages, but here she sits with husband Taher, in majestic splendour on a giant beanbag, wearing a glorious fuchsia-coloured hijab, brighter and gayer than any hijab I've ever seen, and radiantly smiling her toothy smile, despite her horrible news that she's lost the baby. Ever eager to practise his French, Sven sits with them, and listens to talk of their family-run import/export company, how ill-prepared they are to tolerate or be confined by the inefficiency and corruption of North African commerce, and how, happily, their parents gave them money to set up an office in Berlin.

Now it transpires that the only way Karole persuaded Khadra to attend was by assuring her that there'd be no alcohol, but simultaneously she got Mervyn to show up with the promise of vodka. He's snatched it from the kitchen, from where he was instructed it must never stray, and is parading it round the apartment and theatrically offering the Arabs shots. Taher's not happy, and some effort has to be made to separate him from the sybaritic Estonian.

While Sven remains with Taher and Khadra in French, I escort Mervyn back out onto the balcony in English, and am rewarded with a battery of tales from his London life and the days before his got good. Mostly they're about his love life, and a string of boyfriends who accused him of being high maintenance. High maintenance, he thought, sounded like a good thing, so he couldn't understand why they kept leaving him.

On our walk home, Sven tells me how objectionable he found Mervyn, to whose defence I rush. "Why did he offer Taher vodka?" Sven demands to know, "And why did he have to be so camp about it?"

"This is Berlin, not Mecca," I respond. "If Mervyn wants vodka on a Monday evening, let him have it. He's Estonian – he probably needs it. And there's no federal rule against being camp as far as I know – in fact, in certain parts of Berlin, it's compulsory."

Inescapably, we end up re-running the Muslim taxi-driver argument. "They have to learn our ways." "We don't have to shove it down their throats." Etc etc etc. We're so good at it, we know it off by heart.

Sven's overall feeling is that, terrific though they are, my classmates don't "get" me. He's probably right, though I think Karole does a bit. I hope so. She's ridiculously beautiful.

Tuesday 21st June

The campaign has been nasty, brutish and incredibly long. I'm not sure I can stand another two days of it. Show me a reason to be optimistic this morning! There isn't one. There is absolutely no evidence that the Remain campaign is having any impact at all. All I want to read is that Corbyn has praised the EU for codifying human rights, that Cameron has demonstrated that membership ensures a steady economy in a time of peace, and that Farron has spelled out the benefit we all reap from an integration of peoples. But Corbyn's gone AWOL, no one trusts Cameron and Farron's an irrelevance. However, there are plenty of articles warning that everyone's going to be poorer if we Brexit, and plenty of others that dismiss the doom-mongering as 'Project Fear'. A loss of income will do us good, those in the second camp say. There are bigger things at stake than money and growth, they claim. *Sovereignty*, for instance. *Control*. Oh, these meaningless abstract nouns! During the First World War, ten million men died with the word *honour* on their lips, and a decade later, the idea of *honour* had virtually no meaning at all.

The upshot of my obsession with current affairs is a shamefully late arrival in class. Standing in the doorway to Room 204, I attempt to absorb the fact that people aren't where they should be, and all the seats in my section are taken. Roberto shoots me a desperate look. The universe is disordered and there's nothing he can do. With great trepidation I venture across to the far side, settling myself down between the Koreans and Brazilian Melina, and it's from there that I'm introduced to something I've been entirely unaware of until now: the mysterious emanations of Jang-Mi.

To my amazement, Jang-Mi transmits an uninterrupted soundscape of soothing noises. These differ from the usual sounds that provide cover against instructions and questions she doesn't understand, i.e. dithering exhalations that promise the imminent delivery of a flawless answer. These she presumably perfected back home in Korea, where respect for authority is higher than it is here, where I can only assume it's problematical to answer a teacher incorrectly or where "I don't know" is a 'no-no'.

For example, when Jang-Mi is faced with an instruction she doesn't understand, she'll perform an arrestingly high-pitched, breathed "ahhh". It sort of means, 'Ahhh, I see', and it's followed by a pause and then a giggle, the quality and timbre of which is so pretty, so knee-tremblingly beguiling, that all the other women in the class are compelled to echo it and giggle with her – the result being that Almut is enfolded in a veil of feminine tinkling so lovely that she forgets what she wants, and moves on to something else.

That's what Jang-Mi does when she doesn't understand an instruction. When she's confounded by a *question*, she will make a few melodious non-committal sounds with her lips pressed together. Then, as she slowly oscillates her head from side to side and smiles at everyone, the tension builds until one of her classmates cracks and comes up with the answer for her. At this point, she exclaims "*Ach ja!*" with great happiness, as if she herself had been certain of the answer all along, while she graciously extends a magnanimous hand towards the classmate who gave it. Her head tilts indulgently, and on her face a seraphic smile evolves, indicating that she is delighted for her worthy friend to take all the credit.

By comparison, Xiu is less able to defend herself against incoming questions. *Her* speciality is her ability to convey that she's somehow got a question right when she's got it wrong, or, if not right, that she was very close to it – that there was, in other words, some kind of victory for her in the exchange. There's the 'If only you'd asked me a different way' sigh, and the 'I knew it but temporarily forgot it' gurgle, and the 'Oh yes I understood that, but I thought it couldn't be so simple' bleat. She's a six-year-old who hasn't realised that grownups see through that shit. When she's finally given the correct answer, she repeats it, as if time is reversible and we'll all scrub the awkward getting-it-wrong bit.

These self-protective devices are self-defeating because they throw up a barrage of faff which prevents others from helping, or Almut from reposing the question in simpler language. Jang-Mi's is better at deflecting the focus, but Xiu's noises keep the spotlight on her, which is the thing she hates most. If only she would allow herself to admit, "I don't know", then Almut, a lover of stragglers, would cherish her, rather than merely tolerate her. So much of my Asian classmates' efforts go into dissembling, and so little into a genuine attempt to understand whatever is being asked of them, that there's an urgent need for someone to explain that "I don't know" is a perfectly acceptable response in Germany – and that it's as important for meaningful integration as an understanding of Bauhaus or Buchenwald.

What elevates Jang-Mi's soothing noises above her day-to-day coping mechanisms is that they're not mere self-protection. In a kind of saintly, sacrificial act, she comforts the entire room with sounds that rise and fall in pitch and intensity and plot our emotional topography. It's the barely audible whisper of a never-quietening hurricane raging in a far-away land.

Almut poses a question and Jang-Mi gives life to a euphoric little giggle. While the classmate struggles, the pitch of her chuckle rises. As the classmate answers, it deflates to become an anxious and hovering breath. Once Almut accepts the response, the breath swirls with delight. Were she to refuse, Jang-Mi would have several affirming shudders up her sleeve. And there's a whole other range of sounds that she brings into play to accompany our teacher's lengthy monologues, including outright laughs following something jokey or unusual, and murmuring agreement in response to anything social, political or informational. There's outrage, general and theatrical. There's despair and corroboration and sympathy and surprise and revelation, and a whole raft of noises to accompany suspense. She's positively symphonic. To my left, by contrast, Melina slurps coffee for the entire class.

Without attending Karole's party yesterday, Almut must have heard Khadra's sad news, because she announces it to the class. This is shocking but not surprising. Just like she did a couple of weeks ago by broadcasting Roberto's income, she often acts as if she owns us. It's her revenge, I reckon, for all the hours in which she places her own needs below ours – the needs of a bunch of mostly poor, largely unemployed, rootless, German-language-murdering nomads. And should we ever master her beloved language, another load of nincompoops would rush to take up the slaughter afresh. To put us back in our place and show us who's boss, she believes it's her right, whenever she chooses, to make free with our data, however personal. Catching sight of Karole's horrified expression, she twigs that perhaps this time she's overstepped the mark, and smartly flips the subject to yesterday's homework.

During break, Karole and I have a bit of a moan. We moan about Almut's indiscretion, we moan about how the Spanish vegans let her down last night, we moan about grammar and we moan about Brexit. She's happy to hate Farage as fervently as I do, especially the breezy manner with which he bats away questions about what'll happen if Leave triumphs. But when I lay into Jeremy Corbyn's limp performance on behalf of the Remain campaign, she irritably informs me that her Mum says it's almost impossible to get a doctor's appointment in Salford and that's why she's voting 'out'. Then she briskly tilts the conversation to what she did on Saturday night, which was to go out for dinner with her German/Greek pilot partner, Yannis, and two of his German friends, because the truth is that Karole really wants to have a moan about Germans.

Apparently, they had quite a nice time, but their companions were a disappointment. "Oh, why do Germans have to be so boring?" she wails.

Karole thinks they go on and on about things – in the same

way that a Brit might not, or might not be allowed to do. Brits take irony for granted. Unless an Englishman is an actual bore, the social safety net of irony will be deployed. If he becomes too technical or too emotional, for example, someone will skewer the conversation with a bit of a joke or a wryly-worded but nonetheless blatant shift of topic. But in Germany, there's a universally-obeyed rule against interrupting, which precludes the use of the ironic escape route. Interrupting is *verboten*. You may not do it at a dinner party, or in a smoky bar, or even, it transpires, in bed. And this, I suggest, is how Germans acquired their reputation for being relentless and prosaic. The interdiction of 'don't interrupt' is a licence to bore.

Considering that Germans tend to be scrupulously honest, factual and detailed, you can see how a conversation could easily go bad. Sven threw a dinner party to introduce me to his folks, Dieter and Gabi, and invited along a couple of our friends to oil the machinery. We were all getting on very nicely, when, midway through the main course, Gabi asked our chum Bettina what she was up to at work, and Bettina, uninterrupted, answered the question FOR TWENTY-TWO MINUTES, and this was not considered odd.

So I know what Karole means, but I can't allow her to get away with it because I firmly believe it's not on, as an expat, to moan about your hosts. One's job is to understand them. Plus, generalising about Germans, like Karole is gagging to do, and which I persuade her not to do, but which, in my head, I secretly do anyway, is wrong and bad and only half a step away from full-on racism.

Joining us, Mervyn demands to know what we're talking about, and takes my response – that we're trying not to be racist about Germans – as an invitation to be racist about Germans, launching into a stereotyping, cliche-embroidered rant. When I protest, he assures me that he's "not racist actually". If I listen carefully, I will observe that his comments are, in fact, uniquely nuanced. He's not simply generalising about Germans, you see. He's able to speak to the difference between one bunch of them and another. For example, he asserts, Berliners on a good day are direct and no-nonsense but, on a bad day, brusque and offensive. Düsseldorfers are arrogant and superficial, and in Köln everyone's permanently up for a party. Anyway, he concludes, there's no point in not being racist about Germans because they're racist about themselves. Northern Germans are incredibly bigoted about southern Germans and *Wessis* are convinced that all *Ossis* are fascists.

Though Roberto missed Karole's party, his cold's not severe enough to keep him out of class, and when I join him in the coffee shop, he reaches into a pocket, pulls out a crumpled scrap of paper, and unfolding it with the eagerness of a puppy, shares a heavily annotated and coffee-smeared estate-agent's plan of a three-bedroom apartment. Triumph of triumphs, he's finally found himself and girlfriend Francesca a proper home in their new homeland. The place just north of the Landsburger Allee in Lichtenberg looks like a veritable palace, and their idea is to finance it by renting out two of the bedrooms. With boundless, chest-thumpingly-expansive happiness, Roberto insists on paying for my coffee.

When class ends, he invites me and the Koreans to meet up with him and Francesca to eat fish sandwiches and continue the festivities over lunch. Fish sandwiches, he assures me, are a wonderful thing, and surprisingly cheap.

The Maybachufer is the bank of the Landwehrkanal that runs through the centre of town and divides Neukölln from Kreuzberg. It borders a street of imposing, five-story, terraced houses, an avenue of mature plane trees and, on Tuesdays and Fridays, dozens of Turkish stallholders doing a roaring alfresco trade in food, drink, carpets and everything in between.

The fish-in-a-bun things are indeed wonderful. I snag a whole plate of baklava for people to share for dessert, and Roberto treats us to a round of coffee. Squished together either side of a picnic table on a couple of wooden benches that were designed for fewer than our number of bottoms, we're sheltered under the dark trees by the black canal on which a platoon of dazzlingly white swans glide by. We tuck into our feast, our conversation an animated concoction of German, English, Italian and Korean, and everyone has a fabulous time.

...

This evening, Germany plays Northern Ireland at the Parc des Princes in Paris. And what a treat it is. Özil, Schweinsteiger and Kimmich are on fine form, and at the final whistle, we lead the group. (We? Naturally, I'm fully German when Germany's winning.)

Outside school and work, Sven and I have nothing much planned this week so whenever I can tear myself away from the Guardian's front page, there are plenty of opportunities to relax a bit in the evenings, hang out on the terrace or head for a bar. I'm astonished by the extent to which, in the face of a potential cataclysm, normal life goes on as usual, and also somewhat ashamed by my ability to enjoy vast swathes of it.

With celebratory fireworks thumping around the neighbourhood, Sven and I jump on our bikes to make the most of the warm night in Kreuzberg. The bridges over the canal are crammed with uniformly young people. Evidently, it's a particularly German thing to party on bridges, so we avoid them and make for our local watering hole, the pleasantly scruffy Südblock, to mark the solstice with a beer or two. The place is typical of the part of town in which we live: grungy, neighbourhoody and pleasantly mixed – the look Berlin's ex-Mayor Klaus Wowereit called 'poor but sexy' – improvised, impoverished and anti-fashion. Local queer society, small groups of trans people, Turkish couples and gay tourists sit together under strings of twinkly coloured lights. And we do *not* talk about the referendum.

What we *do* do though, is decide to get married! The idea pops out of the second glass of beer, and is greeted with universal glee. "Yes, of course! I was just waiting for you to ask!" I exclaim, momentarily pretending to be a girl, though it's been on both our minds for a while. Whether the UK decides it can or cannot embrace the EU, I firmly believe Sven's the one for me, for now and forever, and I have done ever since the morning after our first night together, when he served me breakfast and literally showed me his etchings. And he's always telling me how he feels the same about me, though, just to prove he's better, he claims to have decided eight hours earlier. The intervening four years have held nothing for us but our happiness (well, ok, we've had one or two days of turmoil, but nothing major, and absolutely nothing lasting), and we're both continually amazed at how brilliantly we co-exist in our perfect little burrow. We want to be together all the time but we're not clingy. We long to share everything with the other, but we allow the other to have his own independence. Considering that we're curmudgeonly old buggers who, before we met, had everything our own way, the whole thing is a major flipping miracle. Our existence is charmed.

So what we agree on is that, one day soon, we'll go to the relevant Standesamt and arrange an appointment for a civil-partnership. We talk about how great it would be if we could get hitched on the next anniversary of our very first meeting. Won't it be fun? We'll keep it small, just us and the obligatory translator. We want to 'leave the church in the village', as the Germans say. Why don't we ask Bettina to be our bridesmaid? Brilliant idea. That's what we'll do.

I always felt I somehow missed out by never knowing the proper way to mark the longest day of the year. Well, now I know. This is definitely how you should do it.

We bike home through streets lined with happy, partying people, holding our secret close, certain we have more to celebrate than anybody else.

Wednesday 22ⁿᵈ June

I'm an engaged man. How exciting is that? While an old international political union looks to be in mortal danger, a new bi-national human one is born! Outstanding! It's like the Christmas episode of Eastenders when Pauline Fowler dies under the festive decorations in Albert Square while, at the same time, Bianca gives birth on the floor of the Queen Vic. As the cosmic significance of last night's decision hits home, a thrilling tingle runs through me. Yet my new situation appears to me reassuringly ordinary, because actually nothing really real has changed. And yet it also feels unreservedly right, thank God. I find myself suddenly and surprisingly more comfortable, safeguarded in a wonderful oasis of security, safely protected from the surrounding desert of swirling uncertainly that is Brexit. And Dad. And the uncertainly of work. And Sven would add the Libyans downstairs, but I wouldn't. In fact, I've 'had an absolute pig', as the Germans would say. It almost puts into perspective the fact that polling in the referendum begins in twenty-four hours' time.

But not quite.

It's going to be ok, it's going to be ok, I chant to myself in a pointless and impotent inner monologue. It is, isn't it? It has to be. But it might not be. And so on.

Thank God for German class. For three and a half hours, I can pretend nothing really important is happening.

Outside school, I bump into Roberto, and I'm just about to share my great news with him, when he shares his bad news with me.

Despite his housing triumph, he continues to be plagued by the worst cold that ever afflicted a human man. More diabolical is his horrible washing-up job in an abysmal restaurant, and, since his Italian doctor ordered him to give up drinking and coffee, his German doctor has instructed him to stop smoking, which is his only hold on happiness. And Francesca's discontentment, he tells me, runs even deeper. Trapped in her stupid dinner-lady job, she craves "more nice things" and wants to travel. "But what sense does that make?" cries Roberto. She was the one who decided to move here, when he was perfectly happy in Sicily. For her, he's dutifully changed countries. For her, he's learning a new language, and for her, he found a nice big flat to live in. And after all that, she wants to travel?! "Where does that leave *me*?" he wails. All this, I'm told, came to a head last night when they switched the blame on each other, and after a large number of Amara Avernas in a local taproom, kept the neighbours awake until one-thirty in the morning by having a screaming fight in the street. Poor Roberto, as Almut would say.

And then he asks me if I've seen Jang-Mi's facebook post. I must have missed it this morning. It reads:

> Wir sind mit anderen Freunden zum Türkischer Markt am Maybachufer gegangen. Wir haben vor dem Tisch zusammen gesessen und Fisch-Kebab gegessen ohne etwas zu sagen.
> Da ging ein alter Mann an uns vorbei, und plötzlich blickte er ärgerlich mich und Woong an.
> Ich habe auch ihn angesehen. Unsere Blicke trafen. Seiner blick hatte viel Ekelgefühl gegen uns, als wenn er die Küchenschaben, die bei seiner Wohnung eingedrungen hatte, fand.
> Das war sehr schwierig aber ein bisschen interessant für mich, weil ich das erste Mal erlebt habe. Ich fühlte fremdartig.

> We went with other friends to the Turkish market on the Maybachufer. We sat together at a table and ate fish kebabs without saying anything.

Learning German (badly)

Then an old man passed by, and suddenly looked annoyed at me and Woong.
I looked also at him. Our gaze hit.
His look had a lot of disgust feeling against us, as if he had found the cockroaches that had entered by his apartment.
This was very difficult but a bit interesting for me, because I experienced the first time. I felt strange.

Firstly, all this misery makes me even more grateful for my own happiness. Secondly, I'm utterly flabbergasted that I perceived none of it yesterday. My memory of the fish sandwich event is that the Koreans joined in as much as anyone else, and that universal joy abounded from overture to curtain call. Neither did I pick up one ounce of the Italian couple's discontentment. What kind of a rubbish observer am I?

Jang-Mi evidently regards the world through a filter of fear I find hard to imagine. I was certainly unaware of any horrible old man creeping along the *Ufer* and giving filthy looks to my classmates. Indeed, it never enters my mind that the occasional unhinged German would like me to leave the country and go back to where I came from. I kvetch about Brexit but whatever happens tomorrow, I'll never look foreign here – something I take for granted on a daily basis.

For my non-EU classmates, living in Europe is not nearly as straightforward as it is for me. Not only the Asians but also, for example, Brazilian Melina has no access to the free emergency medical treatment that I, a citizen of the European Union, am entitled to here. And because they're non-EU, when it comes to jobs, they can't get the ones they want, and find themselves ineligible for the ones they get. A work permit is the stuff of dreams. Insecurity I never have to consider stalks their lives.

All of this comes with the usual caveat. Tomorrow night,

after the polls close, I might suddenly find myself as unrelated to the EU and as precarious as any other citizen of any other third country. For the next forty-eight hours, however, I'm still safe.

For the Arabs and Asians, the obstacles to integration are almost insurmountable. Not only must they deal with an entirely new alphabet and way of reading (letters rather than characters, non-cursive, line-bound, left-to-right), but also the vocabulary is as alien as Japanese would be to me. Moan though I do (and I do), as an Englishman whole tracts of words are guessable and many are identical. 'Interview' is *Interview*, 'job' is *Job*, while 'kidnapped' translates as *gekidnappt*. I gekid you not. For Brits, the pronunciation's hardly a stretch because German spelling is such a reliable guide, especially when compared to the insanity of English – a language that has nine different ways to pronounce 'ough'. 'Cough', 'rough', 'bough' and 'although' to list but four.

Roberto and I head into class where no one's bothered about Brexit at all. Instead, the conversation's all about Karole's crisis. Surrounded by suitcases and inquisitive classmates, she wears a headscarf of a burnished gold colour, which, at first, I assume must be some kind of hijab-solidarity effort. 'Wear a headscarf for Ramadan' or something like that. But no. "Take it off," everyone's urging, while Mervyn rehearses his sadist laugh.

I've never seen Karole look vulnerable, but she seems genuinely upset as she attempts to quell our riotous speculation, explaining that things went horribly wrong when she attempted to dye her hair blond last night. Yannis was a beast and described her as 'a bit of a blonde', and the timing couldn't be worse because, in a few hours' time, the pair are due to fly to Greece where she's to be introduced to his parents. "You're probably making it out to be worse than it is," we chorus. But our concern is fake. We're all gagging to have a look.

Eventually, begrudgingly, she succumbs, and, crikey, she wasn't exaggerating. Her hair's an effusion of acid shades. Patches of bright rust compete with gruesome streaks of banana yellow and scorched brown, and the whole thing is nastily crinkled. But we fall over ourselves to reassure her. It's fine! No one will notice if you don't draw attention to it! "It's lovely," lies Milica. "And if it's a bit wrong, who cares?" adds Letizia, whose hair is never the same colour from one week to the next. Currently she's fizzing-neon-green and wants everyone to call her Lacey. Eagerly, she suggests practical methods of disguising unwanted dark bits to Karole, while I recommend buying a hat. The Arab ladies meet the entire farrago with incredulity and silence.

In an attempt to cheer her up, Almut describes some of her own hair experiments through the eras of punk, post punk, *Neue Deutsche Welle*, electro and techno, when her locks exploded or retreated in line with the city's ever-evolving soundscape. For a moment, I regret missing these celebrated musical revolutions, but I would've been a hopeless amateur had I been here at the time. I didn't like punk in England, so why would I have liked it in Berlin? A huge Bowie fan, if he'd strolled past me on Oranienstrasse, I bet I would've failed to notice. In those days I couldn't understand electro-noise music, and I'm sure I'd have hated all that insane pogo-ing about. The entire scene seemed desperately rough, and not in a good way – just remorselessly hetero.

At breaktime, Karole departs in a whirl of pink luggage, fake Hermes sunglasses, hugs, kisses and her hair catastrophe tightly wrapped up in the golden scarf. I feel a pinch of bereavement, but Mervyn is so distraught that he doesn't know where to put himself. "Call me if you need anything," he shouts after her, about to cry, and shares the rest of the break with Roberto. An unlikely couple: the short, tubby Palermitano washer-upperer next to the tall, golden-haired grieving Estonian buyer. Frodo and Galadriel. I share the news of my engagement with 'Lacey'. Good grief.

After Almut kicks off the second half of class with an annoying lecture about homeopathy (she believes in it, of course), she introduces us to the concept of *Heimat* by asking whether the weather's interesting where we come from. Having listened to her sermonise about curing the oceans with homeopathic remedies for half an hour, we're utterly withdrawn and she gets nothing from us.

Heimat is one of many German words to do with deep feeling for which, extraordinarily, there's no equivalent in English. It almost means 'home' and it almost means 'homeland' – hence it was easy for the Nazis to imbue it with a nationalistic dimension that it doesn't properly possess. What it specifically denotes is the social and physical space that nurtured you, and your attachment to it.

Other wonderful German concepts about deep feeling for which the English have no single word, include *Fernweh* (a longing for distant places) and *Sehnsucht* (an intense yearning for some far-off and indefinable thing). *Geborgenheit* is the feeling that conflates the concepts of 'cosy', 'safe', 'secure', 'warm' and 'being-at-one-with-your-fellows' (what I've been feeling since last night), while *Gemütlichkeit* is the same as *Geborgenheit* but homelier and less profound.

Creating collage is what Sven likes to do when he's not working, and very much with the idea of *Heimat* in mind, he's recently created a series of pieces that merge photographs of nineteenth-century landscape engravings with 1970s, black-and-white, amateur gay porn. Having persuaded a local gallery to show it, we're inviting people to its weekend opening. As my classmates and I mill round our bikes after class, I hand out flyers and am pleased to report that everyone seems quite interested. Roberto is particularly smitten, and closely scrutinises the material. He assures me he'll make sure Francesca knows about it too.

Although our much-longed-for walk seems to be on permanent hold, Roberto has bought me coffee and invited me to the fish sandwich event, so I'm prepared to acknowledge this is the way it goes with him. It's all improvised, and plans shouldn't be taken literally. Plus, if I care to remember my days in Rome, I should know that 'going for a walk' indicates no more than a general desire to hang out together. No actual walking is ever involved.

In the afternoon, I phone *Emma*'s commissioning producer. I've spent the last few days working up my radical and exciting new concept, and I'm now ready to present the idea about Emma Woodhouse as England and Harriet Smith as Ireland in a Brexit-related romantic comedy – a Brexedy, let's call it. I'm sure my employer's going to adore my approach to England's beloved classic, which mixes the kind of radicalism I've observed over here with the traditional values of good old-fashioned English storytelling. I just want to double check, before starting to write the dialogue.

The commissioning producer hates it.

He's shocked by it. Yes, he's actually shocked. Hadn't I realised, he cries, that the whole point of this exercise was to use the book as an excuse for a commercial, period-costume romp? Who do I think the audience is going to be? he asks angrily.

"Well, I hope anyone could – " I begin lamely, but he cuts me off.

"Little old ladies!" he exclaims. "That's who goes to the theatre in the provinces! And little old ladies want to see pretty regency frocks. They want a faithful retelling of a story about girls and boys falling in love. They want Austen's wit and a Mr Knightley who looks as close to Colin Firth as my budget can get. They do not want a story about Brexit! That is precisely the very last thing they want."

He tells me to go away and write what we originally agreed, and to start on it today as the deadline for handing in the first draft is the end of next week.

I have to admit, in terms of the contract, he's right. A traditional adaptation is what we signed on. But what's the point of that? Maybe from an English perspective it works, but from here in Germany, it makes no sense at all. Perhaps I'm really going native.

I sit on the terrace, mulling over his reaction. I wonder how I can ever synthesise the two sides of me – the old English and the new German me. With growing urgency, the two of them demand I choose which to inhabit, and, if synthesis is impossible, I suppose a choice will have to be made. I pray that this setback with *Emma*, this retreat into a reactionary, traditional way of looking at the world, is not a portend of things to come tomorrow.

Thursday 23rd June

On waking, it takes me a few seconds to remember it's referendum day. Once reality hits, the prospect of defeat makes me dizzy. A little devil welcomes the unleashing of a kind of chaos, but my better, if more prosaic angel wishes for nothing but the smooth continuation of everything we have, just as we have it.

Almut's late for class, so Milica and I, the first to arrive, find ourselves locked out, confined to the unlit landing at the top of the stairs. Sporting long, straight brown hair, tiny gold earrings and business-like, tight-fitting, grey trousers, Milica is never unpunctual, invariably on top form and always tries way too hard in class. But she's also surprisingly self-conscious, so she tends to mumble her ever-correct contributions into her hand. Despite her brilliance, I believe Almut hates her because of this meekness, and because of the fact that Milica's life reeks of capitalist contentment and cog-like complicity. Having said that, we've been told almost nothing, except that she's married to stodgy Ostap, has two remarkably un-Ukrainian sounding children (Chase is seven and Max is five) and likes salsa dancing.

Unexpectedly thrown together, she informs me, in her very confident English, that Chase came home from school yesterday sporting glittery red fingernails. This, she assures me, would never happen in the Ukraine, where boys must be boys. But here, kids can be whatever they want to be! And, she merrily adds, grownups can too! Last night her husband splashed out for a babysitter so he could go bouldering and she could salsa in the beautiful old Clärchens ballroom on Auguststraße. "Life is great," Milica explains, "because everybody is middle class. In Ukraine, nobody is middle class. Everybody is very rich or very poor. In Ukraine, my husband make much, much, much, much money because he has good, good job with Vodafone. We are very rich and we do everything we want. But we feel bad because other people cannot do. But in Germany, we are rich like everybody else, and we do not feel bad. In Germany, everybody can do something what they want."

Mervyn turns up to class in time for the break with his head and one arm covered in bandages. Apparently, the story involves drugs and alcohol, but more than that he will not disclose. Mervyn definitely does too much drugs. Off-the-cuff comments in group conversation have often proved him to be a habitué of various gay dance spots, including Berghain, the legendary techno-club, to which, on Friday evenings, vast hordes of Mervyns fly from all corners of Ryanairland to queue round a repurposed energy generating station with a hope but no guarantee of being allowed inside to dance the weekend away. And, however young you are, you can't boogie from Friday night to Sunday lunchtime without a bit of chemical help.

As we stroll towards the coffee shop, he demands to know what I think will happen in England today. Before I have a chance to respond, he's loudly announcing a Leave victory. An English-speaking group forms around us on the pavement, including a bunch of South American musicians from another class and several people I don't know, and together, we listen to Mervyn denounce the British public for losing their minds. He's shocked that the ballot is poised on a knife-edge, especially given the Brits' reputation for rationality. Speaking for his small Baltic country, he's adamant that it's suicidal to leave yourself vulnerable to larger, more aggressive neighbours. "How does Britain think it will go ok alone?"

Roberto insists that it'll all be alright, that the Brits won't do anything foolish, and Milica has heard that the "young people of England" will save the day. According to her, they've registered to vote in droves and of course, will all choose Remain. She's convinced that folk in the UK don't really want "out" given that so many Ukrainians want "in". With part of her country only recently annexed by Russia, she also understands the value of belonging to a bloc whose members treat aggression against one as a threat to all.

Those from lands whose geopolitical reality precludes complacency are genuinely keen to understand the mentality of Leave voters and look to me for clues, their eyes insisting that I must have inside information. But I disappoint them. I'm as far from an answer as they are. I try to explain that I don't think many Leavers actually know what they want themselves. They're less interested in planning the future than in overturning the present. And it's not only the Trotskyite fire-raisers and nostalgia freaks who are in a destructive mood. I inform the group that I'm sure a lot – perhaps a majority – of my countrymen want a change, and that many, unaware of what the EU has contributed to the UK, will use the ballot to make a point about something other than Britain's membership of it.

As we trudge up the stairs back to class, Roberto, sensing my mood, puts his arm round me reassuringly and breaks the news that Francesca, having been informed of Sven's collage show, is as keen as he is to attend.

Reasserting her authority, Almut takes us through *weil* vs. *denn* (because vs. because). But my brain's elsewhere. If it all goes pear-shaped tonight, I'll register my presence with the authorities here, which technically I should have done four years ago, and plough on with citizenship. Will dual citizenship be an option? As someone in his mid-50s, will I qualify for health insurance? Will I even be able to understand the paperwork? I've been trying to get Sven to explain it to me for months. Karole's been filling in forms ever since I've known her, and she still has a way to go. Then, if I manage to conquer it, will I be entitled to access the NHS when I visit England? And God knows where I'd be with tax. Perhaps I'd have to pay it twice, in Berlin *and* London. The whole thing's hideously unsettling, massively flipping tedious, but not, I assure myself for the umpteenth time, impossible.

...

Rather than watch the news and get anxious, Sven and I head for Südblock. But there's no relief to be found. Blithely oblivious to Brexit, every bar in the neighbourhood is showing Austria/Iceland on big screens. Only Südblock has dared to be different by airing some kind of domestic women's game, and this has elicited a gathering of Dykes on Bikes in gargantuan number, which in turn has rendered the alcohol unreachable. So we proceed to our regular standby, Möbel-Olfe, which, thank goodness, is as packed with lush beardy gayboys as ever, and where enormous glasses of Polish Żywiec beer are abundantly available.

By the time we get home, I've miraculously forgotten about the referendum, and, in that moment before Sven turns on the news in the hope that somebody will know something, it's unimaginable to me that things could go wrong tomorrow, or that anything might threaten our newly minted bliss.

Looking unnervingly like regulars from Moe's Tavern and clutching a read-out from their poll, a pair of American psephologists informs the German public that the Remain camp will score a slim victory. Sven seems pleased and wonders why I'm not. We decide against waiting up.

Friday 24th June

Britain has decided to shoot itself, as the Germans would say, 'in the knee'.

Going to class is a ridiculous notion that I countenance for less than a second. I need to stay at home and manically flick between the Guardian, which fuels my misery, and Facebook in search of comfort from friends, or in fact from any like-minded people at all. I need to talk to English people. I need to talk. It takes the edge off the despair that engulfs me. I can't tell whether I'm frightened more for myself, for England, for Europe, or the world in which Brexit accelerates the shift of power away from the West and towards Russia and China. I'm frantic and rudderless.

I phone Mum and Dad to hash it out. The last time I called them in the wake of a national cataclysm was when Princess Diana died, but, as events go, this is on a whole other level. Trying to sound unemotional, I ask Dad how he's doing, expecting him to launch into 'I never thought I'd see the day...', but he doesn't. He's just sad. And he says he's tired, and he's really pissed off about the pills he has to take. Mum's baffled by the referendum result, but too busy to talk for long. She's more concerned to tell me about the pains in Dad's chest. I tell her he didn't mention anything to me about that. Well, he wouldn't, she says. He's used to discomfort, but this is new, and she's worried. She tells me she might get him up to the doctors to see what they think, and I encourage her to do that. So we never really get a chance to share with each other how crushed and hopeless we feel about the political news. I hang up, and make a cup of tea, and try to look for the positives.

But there aren't any.

While Putin and Trump are happy, the victors themselves appear surprisingly downcast. At a press conference that looks about as festive as a hostage video, blazered bigot Farage radiates disappointment and stale tobacco, while Johnson is ashen with terror. Like a dog that runs after a car and catches it, they have no plan for what to do next. Come on, even Baldrick had a plan. But no, it's the government who should've made the plan, they say. In other words, they didn't think they'd win. They didn't even want to win. And their game has been exposed. Whoops.

Cameron, conversely, has a very good plan, and it's to bugger off quick. He resigns shortly after Sven leaves for work. He's created this mess, and someone else can clean it up, thank you very much. What a cock Cameron is, assuming he'd win his sorry referendum campaign because he always wins everything. Millions of lives across Europe will be diminished. The natural course of the UK and the EU is redirected, and not in a good way. A weaker Europe is born, and a discredited England reborn. But he doesn't care. Off he goes, a truly D-list politician. He only wanted to become PM because he thought he'd be good at it. Well, Dave, that just shows you how wrong you can be.

Otherwise, everything's progressing as expected. The pound's plummeted to a thirty-one-year low, three trillion dollars has been wiped off the value of the global stock market (although I have to admit I don't really know what that means), and the Bank of England is forced to commit two hundred and fifty billion pounds to avert some kind of fiscal implosion. That's roughly equal to thirty years of the UK's EU-contributions. Meanwhile, a time bomb is set to explode under the Northern Irish peace process, and Nicola Sturgeon announces that a new referendum for Scottish independence is highly likely (though, to me, that sounds like a good thing – one more entry at Eurovision). Racist demagogue Farage declares that victory has been won "without a single shot being fired", which is a comment that I'm sure will go down tremendously well with Jo Cox's children. Oh, and by the way, he adds, forget about that pledge to spend £350 million a week on the NHS. On sober reflection, it was probably a bit of a mistake.

Learning German (badly)

Many voters admit they backed Leave not thinking their votes would actually count, assuming that Britain would remain in the EU regardless. And it's shattering news to several of my Facebook friends when plenty of people confess that they didn't know what they were voting for. According to Google, one of the most frequently asked questions the day after the referendum is, 'What is the EU?'

Surprised at the extent to which I'm knocked sideways, Sven says that I don't have to come to his *Vernissage* this evening, but how could I not? It's a terrific triumph for him, though with social secretary Karole in Greece, and thus unavailable to phone round and getting everyone's arses in gear, there's no show from any of the classmates. Massively proud of Sven's work, I do my smiley best as partner-of-the-artist. But I'm a zombie inside. Most of my energy's expended in trying not to look at my phone for news.

Though it's a very multinational crowd, there are no actual Brits, so Brexit's no one's top priority, and I'm not given the opportunity to wallow as much as I need. To be honest, it's a relief when it's over and we can get home. Though, almost as soon as we walk through the door, Mum calls to say that Dad's back in hospital.

Not only is there general concern about his new chest pains (though no one's prepared to give it a name or suggest a plan), but his psoriasis has flared up as well, and has colonised previously uncontaminated parts of his body. She's just spent six hours with him in A&E, where, she says, chaos reigned and information was contradictory. I ask how he took it, and she tells me that he's mostly irritated, confused and sure he shouldn't be there at all. Sometimes he seems to know what's going on, but then he'll become disorientated and frightened. After hours of hanging about, they finally put him in a proper ward this evening. The doctor's very nice. He was sleeping when she left. We agree to talk again tomorrow.

Saturday 25th June

Unfortunately, we've got a massively packed weekend, all arranged before anyone thought the world would be collapsing.

At any moment, my twenty-one-year-old godson will be arriving to stay with us for a night, coming from Amsterdam, on his way to Prague through Berlin. Not only that, but Sven's mother, Gabi, is in town for a dance seminar, and wants to see us on Sunday. So I head for the shops to buy enough food to keep everyone going. I'm planning to do *Tafelspitz*!

Immediately on arrival, godson Jack shows off an iffy-looking, Clingfilm-wrapped tattoo that he's somehow managed to get done between the train station and our apartment. My first thought is to phone his mum, but then sanity prevails. So I smile and weasel, "Oh, well done, Jack, that's great". Ghastly tattoo aside, he's a thoughtful guy, and a big Corbyn fan, and he's very happy to discuss what's happening in England, which makes his day with us a cathartic treat for me. We spend hours sitting on the terrace analysing Brexit, until Sven joins us and politely wonders whether I shouldn't show Jack a bit of town since he's got less than twenty-four hours in it. God, I'm selfish.

Once asked, he confesses that he'd be eager to investigate some Second World and Cold War stuff, so I accompany him to the end of our block where a pretty, tree-filled park marks the route the Berlin Wall used to take along Engeldamm. We walk under clear blue skies observing Germany's healed wounds, while fresh new ones are being opened up in England. Jack snaps pictures of people walking their dogs where, only twenty-seven years ago, the death-strip bristled with barbed wire, watchtowers and armed guards. I think about the border between the north and south of Ireland. Will the armed guards be back, and the bombs and the punishments and the endless retaliations, and all the pre-Good Friday agreement horror, just because the ill-informed English "want their sovereignty back"?

Further on, the Wall's course is traced out in a double row of cobbles fixed into the road. It slices across streets, bisects a graveyard and is forced to surrender periodically to new buildings. Usually, it follows the edge of the pavement, looking much like a curb, but occasionally it snakes out into the traffic to lure unobservant cyclists into danger.

By foot, Jack and I follow it all the way to Checkpoint Charlie (now a mecca for tourists), and on to where a section of actual Wall is still preserved near the Martin Gropius Bau, which is a handsome exhibition venue. Sven and I saw Anish Kapoor there, and the Bowie show that did the rounds. I try to bring the old slabs of crumbling concrete to life. After all, young Jack was born after Unification. So I describe the stretch of wall on which a three-hundred-metre-long mural was created by Keith Haring, and invite him to visualise the wooden viewing platforms that were dotted irregularly along the west side. Naturally, there were none on the east. Indeed, when communist-commissioned blocks of flats were constructed in proximity to the border, they were carefully designed so none of their windows faced west. They didn't want anyone getting ideas.

Not far from the Martin Gropius Bau stands the Peking Duck, an averagely tacky Chinese restaurant bedecked with typically bright red and yellow signage. I'm keen Jack sees it for it occupies the site of what was once Hitler's Reich Chancellery. Understandably, he has trouble getting his head round the fact. We stand together on the pavement gazing at the place, trying to imagine Hitler striding into his fortress, leather gloves tucked under his arm, to command a council of war. Neither Jack nor I can conflate the two worlds. Either this is where everything bad happened or it's the place where I live my lovely life in open, friendly, inspiring Berlin. It can't be both.

Jack's gone quiet, but insists he's not averse to seeing more, so we descend into Mohrenstraße U-Bahn station where the walls are richly decorated with vast slabs of red granite, carried there after the war from the Führer's office, or so the story goes. Others relate that the same grand and imposing stone was used by the Russians to decorate their war memorial in Treptow Park. Additionally, I hear it props up the Volksbühne Theatre and lines the foyer of the Humboldt University. I've even been told that it was transported to Moscow to decorate a stretch of subway. Chief architect Albert Speer had the chancellery stuffed so full of it, maybe all these stories are true.

Once Jack's had enough of gazing at granite and going "Wow", we travel further up Wilhelmstrasse, before veering to the left and dodging down an unprepossessing alley, at the end of which we find ourselves standing in the middle of a nondescript car park where groups of tourists mill about with nothing obvious to look at, for this is the spot where Hitler and Eva Braun's bodies were incinerated. Under our feet is the abandoned and now impenetrable bunker in which they holed up while the Soviets were slaughtering and raping their way towards the heart of the city, and the Americans and British were bombing the fuck out of the place.

Having decided against the Peking Duck for lunch, we U-Bahn over to the western district of Schöneberg, and, specifically, Nollendorfplatz for a swift Christopher Isherwood pilgrimage and a visit to the legendary Café Berio. Sitting snuggly at one of its outside tables, we enthusiastically devour their magnificent all-day breakfast as we peruse the weekend world sauntering by. Jack isn't even a bit gay but he's young, bright and well-educated, so he's not averse to learning a bit of queer history, and it's a joy for me to lead him about and show him Isherwood's 1930s playground. So we saunter over to Nollendorfstraße 17, where the writer spent three years working and partying before the city's profligate spirit was expunged by Brownshirts wielding swastika flags, and Nazi terror transformed Europe's most decadent city into a desert of conformity.

Learning German (badly)

Nollendorfstraße 17 is rather impressive with its faded ochre facade decorated with grand white lion heads. Today, use of the ground floor is divided between an antiquarian bookstore and a fetish gear workshop that caters for the queer market. Upstairs, young Christopher spent his Berlin years giving English lessons and working on his brilliant, sardonic tales, immortalising his flatmate Jean Ross and landlady Meta Thurau as Sally Bowles and Fräulein Schroeder in *Mr Norris Changes Trains* and *Goodbye to Berlin*. Round the corner was one of his haunts, the Eldorado, where straight customers would pay to dance with drag artists before attempting to guess their partner's gender, a little like today's Berghain, where half of the thrill for the straights is dancing alongside the leather-clad gay crowd.

At home, both of us exhausted, Jack posts pictures of the Peking Duck on Facebook, while I phone Mum to receive a detailed catalogue of what Dad ate and what he refused to eat, as well as an inventory of the strengths and weaknesses of several members of Teddington Memorial Hospital's nursing staff. I tap on the Guardian and begin to read with horror about Farage's unlovely preening, when Sven politely wonders whether we shouldn't address ourselves to preparing the *Tafelspitz*.

Sunday 26th June

The *Tafelspitz* was a sensation, but there's no rest. After accompanying Jack to the station, we immediately head for Gabi's hotel. My suggestion is to jump on a train and make for Müggelsee, one of Berlin's tranquil lakes, but Sven wants to take his mother to Prinsessengarten, our local flea market, where at this time of year, the Erasmus students sell off their belongings before heading back across Europe and home for the summer break. Gabi's unimpressed with both ideas. She wants to show us her old home.

Obediently, we head to Moabit, which was an inner city, working-class neighbourhood at the time she spent her early childhood there in the years after the war. From the bus stop, we pass a local indoor market, where she says she used to buy her favourite gherkins, and then we round the corner into Bredowstraße. She can hardly be surprised that the place has changed, but she's shocked nonetheless. I can sense her consternation as she lists the transformations. The front door's new, the stucco has vanished, and, naturally, all the names on the bells are foreign to her. Today, the area's the destination for New Berliners struggling to afford an apartment in increasingly-pricey Neukölln. Yet, to her, it still feels like home, she says.

We buzz randomly until someone lets us in, and once through the door, she's quick to point out the original bannisters. Sven and I have a feel of the soft, dark wood. The old ornate floor tiles lie in place, though no doubt they're more cracked than before, and the chestnut tree in the backyard is the same one Gabi used to play under, now of course loads taller. It looks remarkably handsome, and I gaze up through the branches, reflecting on what home is to me, as Gabi remembers the games she enjoyed as a girl underneath it.

I've had so many homes, each one with its own memories

that are as precious to me as clearly Gabi's are to her. As she shows us the door to her old cellar and tells us how frightened she used to be of it, I think about my place in Germany and England. Depending on my mood, I can call either, neither or both home. But can a country be home? A tree and the memory of the games you once played under it – that's home. And I suppose for me, now, Sven is home.

Back on the street, Gabi leads us on a little sniff around the neighbourhood, to discover that the bakery next door has disappeared, along with the *Kneipe* (bar) on the other side of it where the only TV in the street became an excuse for the neighbours to gather. And then suddenly, a hundred different recollections flood through her – the friends down the road with whom her parents were close, who also lost a daughter in the war – a memory of throwing pfennigs down to an organ grinder in the street – the country people who came by with sticks of wood for the fire, and who'd gratefully swap a bundle of timber for a meagre handful of potato peelings – the day her mother told her not to look out of the window, but of course she looked anyway, and there below was the neighbour from the flat above, his body horribly, inexplicably rearranged on the pavement. She remembers being banned from consorting with the *Freie Deutsche Jugend* boys, who were sent in smart uniforms from the East to play jolly band music and lure innocent Western girls into their evil communist clutches.

On the way back, we drop into the church Gabi's parents used to attend, where by chance, a small exhibition has been mounted showing, with maps and photographs, how local Jewish residents were rounded up in an adjacent street, a prelude to far worse elsewhere.

Back at the bus stop, Gabi points out the prison where much of Berlin's antifascist resistance was crushed. With a lowered voice, she tells us that her parents once enthusiastically attended a Hitler rally, but later claimed to be ignorant of everything he did.

From her tone, it's easy to tell she was, and remains, unconvinced by this version of events.

In the evening, we walk to a Greek place by the canal. The food is plentiful and delicious, and tucking into heaps of *dolmadakia* and *dakos*, we discuss Dad. When Sven breaks the news of our plan to get civil-partnered, Gabi's delighted, her first thought to phone Dieter and share it with him.

I try to explain to her what I'm feeling about Brexit and the threat it poses to my situation here. Whenever I open my mouth and utter the word 'dual-citizenship', I feel auras shrivel. Still, she listens patiently to me bang on about insurance and tax and rights of residence, and then tells me I mustn't worry. The British government won't let it happen. She may doubt her parents' veracity, but she has a touching faith in the idiots who run my country.

Monday 27ᵗʰ June

I'm the first to arrive, not exactly buoyant, but eager and determined to improve. Three weeks ago, learning German seemed important, but now the stakes are raised much higher. My old concerns seem theoretical by comparison since the whole thing's gone nuclear. Learning German is now an absolute necessity.

But this positive mood is almost immediately challenged by Milica who tells everyone who'll listen that Brexit is the push to make all the dominos tumble, that it has probably wiped out the Ukraine's shaky chances of joining the European club, and that, according to her accusing eyes, it's all my fault. But other classmates are kinder, and there's a lot of touching of the arm and shaking of the head. Not for the first time, I wish Karole wasn't in Greece. In contrast, Xiu seems unusually sunny.

Roberto's very sorry that he and Francesca weren't able to come to Sven's collage show on Saturday. He assures me, however, with three days off work and a heat wave predicted, he's going to make the most of it by lying in the park drinking pastis. Great. That'll do him good.

Everyone seems fractious in the baking heat. Snappish Almut accuses us of being lazy and hopeless as we struggle to concentrate. Impatiently, she abandons one exercise after another because she doesn't think we're getting them, and we totally are, or at least we are to the extent that we ever get anything. Mervyn confesses to having the worst hangover of his life after a weekend that began at the Christopher Street Day Parade and ended in hell when, once again, he blanked out, smashed his phone and mislaid fifty euros. An argument between him and Mira about gay parades swiftly ignites. Almut scolds Leila for not listening, chastises Xiu for burying herself in her phone and responds ungraciously to stellar contributions from Milica and Letizia. There's no mention of Brexit. Instead we discuss rivers.

Almut: *(to Xiu)* What is the Rhine?
[Pause]
Xiu: *(whispers)* The.
[Pause]
Almut: What...is...the...Rhine?
[Long silence]

After I've presented a little speech entitled 'What I did on my holidays', Jang-Mi wants to know about Sri Lankan trains, but I think she's asking about food and so I go on at great length about curry. Prepositions continue to be an absolute bugger. Everything morphs around them in terrible ways. In fact, last year I decided that trying to master the fuckers wasn't worth the misery. So what if I use *zur* instead of *zum*. But then I heard racing driver Felipe Massa announcing in English that he was "very much looking forward for Silverstone in two weeks' time", so I immediately resolved to conquer the goddamned things and not surrender until I had. Yet here I am once more, suffering brain-fade and willing coffee time to come and put an end to my misery.

As we prepare to head home, desperate to get out into the fresh air and the sun, Roberto asks for permission to speak to the group. The refugees, he solemnly informs us, don't need clothes any longer. They have shelter and no one's going hungry. But they're in desperate need of electronic equipment – phones, computers, anything like that. Please don't bring things to school, he advises. We should take our old tech gear directly to the collection points. There are two – one miles away in Spandau, the other in nearby Neukölln. When we request the Neukölln address, Roberto can't remember it, but he assures us that he will have it for us very soon.

...

The news from Teddington is that there's no news. Dad undergoes daily tests, is made to walk up and down, and is reluctant to eat anything but crème caramel. When I ask if Mum would like me to come over, she tells me categorically not. There's no need. Pam-across-the-road is on hand to help. Unless anything radically changes, we'll discuss it again when her supportive neighbour leaves for a vacation in a fortnight's time.

I use my weekly bout of tandem with Jana to explain to her that, over the weekend, though billed as advisory, the referendum has miraculously, and against all sense, become binding. Thirty-seven per cent of the electorate, or twenty-seven per cent of the population want it, so we're doing it. To me, the whole thing doesn't feel much different from a coup.

A lunatic fringe idea has been allowed to establish itself as political orthodoxy. Because Johnson and Gove allied themselves to Farage's bigotry, the unspeakable has become speakable. Through their sinister campaign, hate has become normalised. Grown men shout racist comments at ten-year-olds in the street, football hooligans threaten queers in Covent Garden, the doors of the Polish Centre in Hammersmith stand daubed with xenophobic graffiti and Muslims across the country are instructed by emboldened bigots to pack their bags and get out.

Jana's baffled. Despite the fact that, as usual, I'm going too fast, politics is such a grown-up affair in Germany. She asks how it can be that Farage and Johnson have been allowed to get away without having a plan? But even that, I assure her, is not the crux of the issue. The important point is that no plan will ever work without diminishing both the UK and the EU. Brexit is impossible, at least on the terms by which it was sold. The British people have been lied to. Of course, most politicians lie most of the time, but the Leave argument, I inform my open-mouthed friend, was comprised exclusively of Very Big Lies Indeed, and Farage's victory ushers in an age of demagoguery.

The timer pings. Forty minutes have elapsed, and, as usual, I've been entirely self-serving, taking my poor abused tandem partner hostage and shouting at her. God knows she's got enough problems of her own. Switching to German and thus robbed of ninety-five per cent of my vocabulary, I finally ask her how she is, and enquire whether her week has been as traumatic as mine, fully expecting her to assure me that the drunk husband has smashed all the glassware and the daughter's run off to the circus. But it transpires that things are looking unusually promising in Janaland. The spouse hasn't consumed anything more malign than fizzy pop since last we met, and Jana thinks she might have found someone to lend her a decent chunk of money to help launch her kids' cookery school – an old girlfriend who's made a ton of dosh in telecom-something-or-other.

When I arrive back home, Sven struggles to give me the attention I think this amazing news deserves. He's gripped by events at the Euros – specifically the England/Iceland post-match interviews. A tiny north Atlantic island has knocked the English out of the contest. Thus, manager Roy Hodgson, the only British leader with a decent idea of how to exit Europe, has overseen a kind of sporting Brexit.

Albion has taken back control of its destiny to prove itself a strong and self-sufficient powerhouse, and lost a football match to a country with a population smaller than Sunderland's. Burn! as the social media generation might put it.

Tuesday 28th June

I spot Karole by the bikes. Returned from Greece, she cuts an outrageously striking figure. Her spellbinding accessories jangle seductively as she waves hello. After sharing a mandatory WTF about Brexit, we merrily trot up the stairs to class, frantically discussing Johnson, Gove and Farage, and apportioning blame. Her brown skin glows with health and, most crucially, her hair, held back with a wide, ivory-white alice band, has made a miraculous recovery. I'd certainly be prepared to remain on the landing and miss five minutes of German in order to hash over with Karole the resignations of sixty-five Labour frontbench MPs and the vote of no-confidence in Corbyn their departure has triggered. But Karole suggests we discuss it after class, and propels us into Room 204, where a big fuss is made, and all the girls hug her.

Despite the serial crises facing Greece, from debt to refugee, the ancient land remains an unencumbered paradise, according to Karole. Notwithstanding Brexit, she and Yannis had a superb time (his Greek parents love her – of course). Plus, she's received a text from a boutique handbag shop with an offer of a so-called mini-job, and she reports with great pride that she'll start work this afternoon. I suppose it's reasonable for her to be more excited about her job than about Jeremy Corbyn's prospects. Of course it is. But I'm struck by the difference in our perspective. To her, if she thinks about it at all, Brexit's something that happened the day she got offered her new job. To me, however, it's a political catastrophe and a personal disaster. She's well on her way to becoming a German. I work for an English producer. I'm not even considering looking for a job in any of Berlin's theatre, while Karole will be selling handbags in German to Berliners. I speak English at home while she at least tries to speak German to Yannis. She's got this far with one teacher in six months. Almut's my sixth teacher in as many years. Brexit's a sideshow for Karole.

Nevertheless, if I'm to make sense of a life in Germany, I have to pass this module, do the next and the next and the next, and pass the exam at the end of it. But when Almut produces a bunch of multi-coloured, multi-sized pieces of paper and pins them up in a row, I see nothing but failure. This nasty snake of seventeen segments, filling the entire length of two white boards, details various parts of speech to help us construct proper grown-up German sentences. And we must learn, practice, perfect and, from now on use ALL SEVENTEEN OF THEM, AND IN THE RIGHT ORDER, when we speak and write. Thank God no one told us about this is A-1-1. We'd have all run away.

While we queue for coffee, Almut kindly enquires how I'm feeling. Without a thought of trying it in German, I tell her how appalled I am about Johnson's higher than high-handed suggestion that Britain could remain in the single market without obeying any of the rules – an idea that prompted Angela Merkel's observation that there'll be no cherry picking once Article 50's triggered. He may want his cake and eat it, but as the Germans would say, 'you can't dance at two weddings simultaneously'.

"Why would the English people do such a stupid thing?" Almut demands to know, looking at me, not as Tim, but as an embodiment of all the evils of my home country – the football hooligan in Marseilles, the bellicose UKIP politicians who'll let the Syrian refugees rot in camps because they can't be bothered to help. Today, I wear my Englishness as a badge of shame.

"Ah, well," she shrugs. "Perhaps you were never really in Europe anyway."

After class, I find my bike entangled with Tracey's, and as she and I pull them apart, she calls me David and asks if I can recommend a local gym to her. I certainly can, and once I've reminded her my name's Tim, I do. The gym I recommend, and not for its name, is McFit. It was born when fashion dictated that all low-cost services must be called Mc-something, like the hideously named McPaper stationary shops, and the witless McPark at

Learning German (badly)

Tegel Airport. Tracey doesn't seem entirely satisfied with my advice, but she has no more questions, so I clamber onto my bike and bid her a cheery, "See you tomorrow". Suddenly she's blocking my path. "I don't understand the others," she blurts out, trembling.

It's true, she understands no more than Xiu, and she still falls back on English when confused. If she does try German, it comes out with such a strong Irish accent that no one can understand. After Mira's classroom-based birthday party, Karole and Tracey shared washing up duties downstairs in the school's kitchen. Wiping chocolate cake off Almut's plastic spoons, Tracey was happily chatting away – largely in German – when Karole put down her tea towel and grabbed the Irishwoman's arm. "You know what, Tracey?" she said, "You shouldn't be insecure about your German. It's good. You know a lot. But you have to understand that you've got to try and pronounce it with a German accent!"

Tracey has me pinned, and looks like she's about to cry.

"Oh, no, neither do I," I say. "I don't understand everyone at all. Especially the Spanish speakers."

"No, and I can't understand Mira", she adds.

Obviously Cuban Mira is one of the Spanish speakers, but I let it pass.

Somewhat soothed by my admission, she steps back.

"Honestly, we're all as bad as each other," I lie. "Everyone's struggling. Just keep showing up."

She looks mystified. How can just showing up be the answer when you understand nothing? I sympathise with her, I really do. "We're all in the same boat. You can do it."

She nods, her face full of fear. "See you tomorrow," I say, as gayly as I dare, and push off.

I should take her for a cup of tea, shouldn't I? But I tell myself I must go home and try again with *Emma*, though the truth is I haven't been able to do a stroke of work on it since the day before the referendum when my commissioning producer hated all my ideas. Anyway, if I'm honest, my sympathy is limited. Tracey's Irish.

Whether she passes the exam or not, she'll remain in the EU. If anything, *I* should be the one asking *her* for advice and help. Brexit changes everything for me, and for the UK too. Failing to remain in the union triggers a self-imposed exile from power for the country that, a-hundred-and-fifty years ago ruled the world. In the future, Ireland, as part of the EU, will have more sway over global events. Across the Irish Sea, a thousand-year-old balance of power is shifting fast. And this time, for the first time, Tracey's on the winning side.

...

In the evening, I catch a wonderful BBC documentary about a reunion of key players involved in the making of the 2012 Olympic opening ceremony. It's certainly comforting to look back to that celebrated summer evening in London, when it seemed that the country was willing to think honestly about itself and its history, when it celebrated the NHS and honoured the Windrush generation. I remember experiencing a faint stirring of patriotism for the first time in my life.

Danny Boyle's party was the greatest warm-up act ever staged, including the most complex scene change in history. And the delight of it was that, with thousands of volunteers as its engine, the night seemed not to be about nation states competing against each other, but, instead, about inclusion. It managed to celebrate what Britain's given to the world rather than what it's taken, and, for once, unabashed and unselfconscious, England revealed itself in all its creative quirkiness without any recourse to jingoistic posturing.

To me, the documentary is a reminder that the country, for all its faults, can sometimes get it right, and as I become increasingly engrossed in it, I find myself simultaneously smiling broadly and crying.

For a moment we had it, I think. And now we've thrown it away.

Wednesday 29th June

Working on the concept of 'should', we're tasked with writing a letter. We must invite a classmate to our homeland and give them advice about what to do there. 'You should do this, you should do that', etc. For example, I pen a paragraph about the UK, with absolutely no reference to referendum-related issues, for Milica, while Felipe urges me to come to Uruguay, and Leila's job is to invite Letizia to Iraq. Inspecting our efforts, Almut finds that solipsistic Mira has misunderstood the brief and written a letter about Cuba to herself. Next to her, Leila sits staring at a blank sheet of paper. "Why haven't you put anything down?" Almut enquires. "My advice to Letizia is not to go to Iraq," Leila explains, avoiding Almut's eye. "She should stay here."

A new world characterised by chaos, incompetence, schism and political self-harm may be emerging in England, but nothing's as bad as Iraq. I should keep things in perspective. But I can't help it; I'm angry and desperate. Exactly at the moment I need to concentrate in order to get German under my belt, I don't have the space in my brain or my soul to engage with it. Not only have I abandoned *Emma*, but I've done no German homework since last Friday. Class shenanigans seem utterly unimportant. The lesson is various shades of bullshit. Almut's stupid, the class is stupid, I'm stupid. I'm lost, I'm slipping, I'm sunk.

I wonder if there's a better way to learn the language than this. I try reassuring myself that I'll catch up in the summer break. But will I? Not if I'm as profoundly disenchanted as I am now. It feels as if I'm experiencing a perverse, self-harming urge, out of sympathy with my country.

What happened to the idea that it would be lovely to be a student again, striding happily into class and osmotically becoming German? I realise I'd been living in a Golden Age. I could go where I wanted, pick up some of the language and pretend to be local. But that world is dead. It was a pipe dream. The pretence is over. A new world has been born and fresh rules haven't been written yet. Cast adrift in a shit creek of uncertainty, what do I do? I panic. I've been panicking since last Friday, and it's only getting worse.

"Why does it take so fucking long to learn a language?" Mervyn brays, as we hit the pavement at break time. But when it comes to bellyaching, Karole's got bigger fish to fry. Arriving at the handbag shop yesterday, they gave her three minutes to eat her lunch and steam her shirt, then made her stand around in heels on the shop floor for six hours without a break, because, in a mini-job, the break's triggered at the six-hour mark. She's thirty-four years old, she cries, with loads of experience in fashion and business. In New York, she used to earn a-hundred-and-twenty-thousand a year. As a handbag seller, she'll nett seven hundred a month. There, she would have spent that on a bag without thinking. Here, she's selling them to the sort of bitch she used to be there. Karole's self-image of an American model-slash-business woman collides with Berlin shop-girl, and explodes into a million pieces.

Heading off in the direction of her bike, she tells us she intends to miss the second half of class so that at least she can have a proper lunch break this time, but Mervyn won't let her go. "Listen," he says, "I've unfriended Letizia!" "Why?" we chorus. "Because I don't enjoy being constantly made to feel disgusting for not being a vegan, that's why." And he launches himself on a highly enjoyable rant against the tattooed ones. (These classes have made none of us any nicer.) He often bumps into them in the supermarket, he tells us, but only ever by the shelves where out-of-date stuff is sold off cheap. "They can't be poor," Karole says. "Tattoos cost a lot." But Mervyn reckons their ink work's done by friends. "Have you seen her 'Hello Kitty' abortion?" he asks. "It looks like a rash." He sticks two fingers in his mouth and pretends to vomit.

Learning German (badly)

Karole finally makes a break for it, leaving me with Big Baltic Boy, who immediately embarks on a monologue about his latest trip to KaDeWe (Berlin's Harrods). It's not my fault right now that he's the only person in sight who can understand enough English for my purpose. I need him to be a conversational punch bag while I try to clarify what's happened in England, and why. Listing the causes and itemising who's to blame helps me feel less insane. And, if I can understand it, perhaps then I can live with it, or even start to see where we might go next.

"Go on then," he nods unenthusiastically.

"Ok. This is what I've got so far... Inequality is rampant. The north is full of empty towns and shuttered shops."

"Who wants to live in the North anyway? Why don't they just move?"

He may have a point but I'm determined not to be derailed. "The elite are ignorant and complacent. No one's bothered about lifting people out of poverty. Everyone just talks about identity politics, but most people feel alienated from that –"

"I don't. You don't." When did Mervyn get so sharp?

"Wages have flat-lined and chances receded," I continue. "Globalisation makes a mockery of having any pride in labour, and the idea that, if you work hard enough, you can be whatever you want isn't true anymore."

"It's true for me."

"Sure, for people like us, ok. We up-sticks and go where we want. But not everyone runs around the world like us. Many people feel their identity – their white, British identity – is under threat."

"Hah! So identity politics is ok when it's about them, then?"

I ignore him. "They don't care over much about freedom of movement. They can't tell the single market from a customs union. But they fear the idea of a country called Europe, and when the question on the ballot paper offers the illusion that they can protect their English identity, they grab it."

"They're all racists in other words," snarls Mervyn, who, having lived amongst them, should know.

"Fifty-two per cent of them?"

He shrugs, suggesting, 'Why not?' "But it's not just working-class people who voted for Brexit, is it?" he asks. "It wasn't only Newcastle. Posh places voted 'out' just as much."

Of course he's right. 'Posh' Wiltshire and Hampshire voted Leave, while 'working-class' Liverpool and Leicester chose Remain. And yet Corbyn's lost his no-confidence vote because of the way he failed to sell the idea of staying in the EU to the party faithful. The figures suggest he did no worse than any other leader.

"Maybe it's more to do with everyone's disillusionment with the government," I suggest. "The illegal war in Iraq. The way the Conservatives propped up the banks after the 2008 crash. The war gave us refugees, and the crash gave us austerity, and isn't that what people voted against? And let's not underestimate the influence of the right-wing press's world-beating xenophobia, and the EU-lies it's spouted for decades. 'Euro notes will make you impotent', 'Circus performers must wear hard hats', 'Cows must wear nappies'. Not to mention Farage's naked stoking of racism, and the media's decision to cast him as a clown rather than a mortal threat. And how significant are the data-harvesting people at Cambridge Analytica and their attempts to make electoral fairness a thing of the past? Then there's the country's refusal to relinquish its misremembered history – oh, and my mother told me that my cousin's wife's father voted for Brexit because his best mate's son is training to be a doctor and he hates the Health Secretary who campaigned for Remain. So? Mervyn? How's that? What do you think?"

He's finished his cigarette and wants to return to class, but I stall him. "Does all that sound right?" I demand. "Have I missed anything?" But he looks at me wearily. The truth is he's still coming down from the weekend. "See you later," he says, winks and walks off.

Learning German (badly)

...

Suspecting there had to be a better way of enjoying the Eurovision Song Contest than through the filter of Terry Wogan's casual racism, in 1991 I decided to attend it as a live event. Staged in Cinecittà's Studio 15 in Rome, it was the first time that Germany took part as a reunited country, and the last time Yugoslavia submitted a song. The ex-communist federation was falling apart. Europe was in one of the greatest states of flux it had ever experienced, and the politics were fascinatingly shadowed by those of Eurovision.

Apart from the song contest and all its glories, another thing that particularly struck me during my first visit to Rome was something I noticed while sightseeing in the Forum. Affixed to the wall near the entrance of the capital's ancient ruins, I spotted a series of maps made of plaster, or perhaps concrete. They graphically chart the growth of the Empire from its beginnings as a city-state to the pan-continental monster it became a few hundred years later. I was already familiar with the shape of the continent as Charlemagne settled it, and could recognise maps proscribed by the victors in Vienna, Versailles and Yalta. I knew what Europe was as defined by the EEC, as it still was then. But I had no idea that, at the midpoint of its expansion, when Hadrian was Emperor, Roman Europe claimed almost the same territory as the EBU, the European Broadcasting union, and producer of Eurovision.

A year later, I finished writing my first play and called it 'EuroVision'. It opens with a scene between the Emperor Hadrian and his lover Antinous who are celebrating the settled peace of the known world by launching a pan-Empire song festival, and it ends in the present-day when the Spanish contestant in Eurovision is taken hostage as a punishment for not coming out, and tied up in a closet by Gary an English box-office clerk and his boyfriend Kevin the trolley-dolly. I won't bore you with the details of what happens in between, but I'm glad to report that, on the fringe, the gay romp and gentle satire on European union was something of a success. It even transferred into the West End for a short run.

Another continental trip inspired my next play. This one looked at Britain's rocky relationship with its European partners from a more recent historical perspective. Beginning with the early days of the Coal and Steel Community, it moved via de Gaulle and his serial refusals to let us in, to Heath's triumph and Thatcher's Euroscepticism. The starting point for it had been an inspirational visit I made to the village of Schengen in Luxembourg, where the idea of European-wide, border-free travel was first given voice. Coming from Germany, you cross a bridge into Luxemburg, pass through Schengen, and, after three hundred metres, turn left. Now you're in France. Three minutes – three countries. That experience was the germ of the play, which, perhaps because it concerned itself with issues of European integration, wasn't exactly a smash hit, but it was produced.

I was trawling through Norman Davies magisterial book *Europe* when I found the inspiration for a third play on the subject. On page 994, Davies writes about the Pan-European League – a precursor to the EU, which sprang up after the First World War with pacifism and federalism at its core. One of the League's first offices opened in Tallinn, Estonia. Outside the door was a brass plate with the inscription PANEUROPA UNION ESTONIA. When the Soviets invaded seventeen years later, the plate was hidden by the League's members. Davies writes that in 1992, during a visit to Estonia by Dr Otto von Habsburg (the doyenne of the European Parliament), it was brought out of hiding and presented to him – as a symbol of Estonia's hidden aspirations. At the time, supporters of the USSR were claiming that Estonia was too small to be a feasible independent state but, nevertheless, the would-be-republic declared independence, joined NATO and the EU, and then won the Eurovision Song

Contest too. ('Everybody' by Tanal Padar and Dave Benton, 2001, 198 points.)

The play that these events inspired told the story of the Baltic countries' 1989 protest against its overlord, the Soviet Union, during which about two million people joined hands to form a human chain that stretched nearly seven hundred kilometres across the three European republics. The protesters faced east, towards Moscow, and, despite the direst of warnings, no shot was fired. Two years later, the USSR was a thing of the past.

Now I feel it's time to write another European play, and I don't need to go anywhere or read anything to find my inspiration. There's enough to be mined from the events of the last week. In terms of narrative, I'll turn once again to Britain's disastrous relationship with the continent, this time beginning with Blair's Europhilia and the right-wing's reaction to it, and ending with Hannan's cunning, Cumming's deviousness and Farage's bile. I've no idea yet how to corral all that on to the stage, but my experience is that anger gets the creative juices flowing nicely, so it shouldn't be too hard.

Thursday 30th June

The heavily sought-after green bench outside the coffee shop seats three at a squeeze. Mervyn (rebandaged), Almut and I are merrily squished into it (me in the middle), when Almut decides to tell us how the tectonic plates of geopolitics have played out over the years in Room 204. She begins with present-day Syrians and Spaniards, and works back to some switched-on Israeli and Palestinian students who battled each other through a challenging series of modules. She recalls the English woman who cried when her brother got sent to the Falklands, and the young Balkan men transported to Germany in the '90s by families already established here.

Naturally, the parents wanted to shield their sons from Yugoslavia's bloody war, but the men themselves often longed for combat. According to Almut, one in particular became so impassioned during a political discussion in class, that he stood up from behind his desk, gave the Nazi salute, and yelled "*Heil Hitler*". Almut quickly reassures us that, without thinking, she responded to this horror by yelling a fierce "*Raus!*" at him, pointing firmly to the door.

Then she wonders if I know that Karole once took part in the Miss Universe competition as Miss Botswana. "Really?" I enquire breathlessly. I had no idea. But we get no further, because Mervyn interjects and, in a highhanded tone, instructs Almut, "Actually, that's not something Karole wants everyone to know."

At home, in the cool, dark study, I turn my back on yet one more in a seemingly endless succession of fabulous summer days, in order to spend the afternoon online following events in London. But first, for a bit of light relief, I check out Miss Universe, and it's true – Karole did compete for Botswana! And she did well too, coming first equal with Miss Nicaragua and Miss Vietnam in national costume, third in swimsuit, twelfth in evening gown, and sixth overall. What a feat. What glamour. I'm in awe.

Emma is in a forlorn state. I'm about to miss the first-draft deadline, yet I can't motivate myself to even look at it. The referendum result has changed everything. Who cares about literary romance when a Tory leadership battle is drawn? Anyway, I'm still sore about the fact that the producer hated my concept. I decide the best thing to do is to phone him again, and tell the truth. Though it's heart-breaking to admit, the world is obviously regressing. Clearly this is not the time for a radical reimagining of an English classic. What he's asking for at least has the virtue of being very easy to do. Enough with the thinking, Tim. Just get on with the retyping. Clearly, when I'm working for England, I shouldn't try to be German. I'll concede defeat and ask for a four-week extension.

He's pleased I've come to my senses and is surprisingly sympathetic about the fact that I have nothing to show him. He's done little himself since the 24th, he reassures me, beyond staring open-mouthed at his computer, ringing friends and howling at the moon.

Sometimes I feel like a freak for getting so upset by the news, so I find his response hugely reassuring, and together we gleefully race through the leadership contenders, competing to be the most outraged by Stephen Crabbe (whom we write off because of his connections to gay cure groups), Theresa May (who tackled illegal immigration by sending buses round the country with 'GO HOME' written on the side) and Gove, that "Maoist who's gone a bit barmy" to quote his friend, the out-going prime minister, Cameron. Euphorically, we marvel that the clear favourite, Boris Johnson, is not on the list at all – the reason being that Gove, in a spectacular act of fratricide, declared him "unready to lead"! What's more, Johnson himself has agreed with this verdict! Regretfully, Boris can't be the one to take the country out of the shit in which he's landed it. Despite the fact that he and his confederates have created the greatest constitutional crisis since the 1680s and cost us our membership of the EU, like his mate Dave before him, he gets to walk away from the scene of his unforgiveable crime and leave others to mop up the blood.

We avidly hash out who's the biggest shit of them all, and swiftly come to the conclusion it's Gove. He saw Johnson's opportunism and raised it with his weapons-grade treachery. Gove must be king himself.

...

Bettina's rescheduled me for this evening, but there's no poem to study. We're just going to chat in German. No doubt, we'll labour for as long as I can think straight (or as long as she can put up with it), then revert to English and open a bottle of wine.

Staying in my own language, I answer her question about my progress in class. Tomorrow will be the last day of the current module, I tell her, and I feel like I'm failing. It's going to take me so long to learn German that, by the time I get there, I'll have no memory left, and the whole thing will have been pointless.

"But you can't fail!" she responds, outraged at my cavalier attitude, "You need to get citizenship, don't you?"

"I do, I do. But, honestly, Bettina, the VHS has slayed me. I'm sure my German's getting worse."

"Of course it's not."

"To be honest, I don't really know whether it's the right school for me any longer."

"So what are you going to do?"

"Find somewhere else, I suppose."

"Aren't they all the same? And nowhere is cheaper."

"Cheapness isn't the only criterion."

"You're so middle-class."

"You can hardly accuse me of being middle-class!"

"You're the epitome of it!"

Oh dear. Bettina's in one of those moods.

Learning German (badly)

"You want to throw cash at the problem. But that's not learning the language, that's just spending money. You have to work at it."

"I work! I work!" I squeal. "I've learned a lot in theory, but I practise so little. We just go round the room grinding out answers to lifeless questions in a textbook. We lack sunshine. We lack sleep. We're anaemic and stupid. Maybe it's me. I'm definitely worse at learning languages than I thought, and I never thought I was any good."

"But last time we talked about the course, you loved it."

"That was four weeks ago."

"So what happened?"

For Bettina's benefit, and to lighten the mood, I list the ways in which everyone annoys me, from Almut's time-wasting, her indiscreet revelations of our secrets and her need to amuse us and make us love her to Khadra's pontificating and Mira's shouting, the vegans' proselytizing, and Fairuz who laughs at grammar. I tell Bettina that even Milica's started to piss me off with her relentless straight-laced-ness. And no one's seen Roberto since coffee break on Monday. People say that he's gone to the dark side and moved into Köpi, the squat round the corner. And Mervyn, though hilarious in spurts, is a one-trick pony. None of his funny lines adds up to an actual conversation. And Karole might be good and glamorous and bold, but she can be grand and superficial as well. And then there's Xiu...

I chronicle the doodling, and I report the rustling. And I demand to know from Bettina if she could concentrate on learning a language when, next to her, a small Chinese teenager spends her class-time intently scratching a tiny scrap of paper with an ancient stubby pencil. Today, Xiu wasted the entire first half of class sketching a diminutive man bounding across hilltops (there were miniature clouds and trees), holding aloft a placard bearing Chinese characters. It was all horribly 'Cultural Revolution', and as soon as she was happy with it, she rubbed it out and drew it again.

I tell Bettina about the little tray Xiu made from another miniature fragment of paper in the second half of class. Smaller than a matchbox, I thought it couldn't possibly serve a purpose, though it was neatly done.

And then the rustling started. She rustled as loudly as she'd ever rustled before. First, she produced a packet of Haribo sweets and rubbed it for ages between her fingers. It was the tiniest packet of sweets in the whole world but my goodness, it made a fine noise. When she finally opened the packet, all the sweets miraculously fitted into her tiny paper tray!

Seriously, I wanted to kill her. Instead, I made a mental note never ever to visit China.

I can't help noticing that Bettina's reaction to my merry tales about the agony I suffer is not the one I was hoping to inspire. In fact, her unamused face is fixed in a grim expression of disdain. She tells me that she thinks I sound grand when I talk like this, and that I pontificate far worse than Khadra ever could. She says she recognises me in the Almut I describe – that I'm as desperate for a laugh, and as condescending and as patronising too. She tell me I'm just like Fairuz who makes grammar a joke. After all, instead of going home to revise what I've learned, I must spend the afternoon typing up skits about everything and sharing everyone's secrets, not only to the class, but to any stranger who might buy this book, should it ever see the light of day. So I'm indiscreet on a far more dangerous level than Almut.

There's no derailing Bettina from her mission to call me on my faults. In fact, far from being the broad-minded, inclusive world traveller I like to imagine I am, according to her I'm a sexist and racist monster.

"I'm not racist!"

"You sound it."

"But I'm not making any of it up. Is it my fault that people are a walking vindication of national stereotypes?"

"Tim, you have violent thoughts against young women."

"I do not!"

"You said you wanted to kill Xiu."

"Well...I didn't mean I actually..."

"It's what you said! I know you're not really like that. But I can't like you, I mean the 'you' in class that you tell me about."

This is a bit of a blow.

Defending Xiu against my murderous attacks, Bettina says that the Chinese woman sounds like an attractively self-contained and self-sufficient young person. She obviously doesn't need people laughing at her jokes all the time. And her advice is that, instead of mocking her, I should emulate her. In fact, she challenges me to celebrate Xiu's rustliness, to admire it and to love it.

And then, finally, she opens the wine.

I grasp the glass she offers, and drink too fast.

One of the reasons I've spent so much of my life outside England is to distance myself from English racists. I learn languages partly to explore and celebrate difference. I keep a diary to showcase and legitimise cosmopolitanism. I write about my classmates because they amuse me but also to demonstrate that we're all the same. But Bettina would probably say I've failed to achieve any one of these gaols.

"You may be right about all that, and I'll give it some thought, I will, I promise," I begin. "But, seriously, racism aside, it's hard for me right now, Bettina. It's not simple to possess a steady heart and a focussed mind for learning German, given the absurdly precarious position I find myself in."

"You're about to marry a man with a university job who, in a few years' time, if nothing goes wrong, will be in possession of a German government pension. You are not in 'an absurdly precarious position.'"

"Ok, ok, I'm not an indigent refugee. But again, that's not my fault. Just like all the other million-plus Brits in Europe, I'm lost in a kind of limbo here." When Article 50's triggered, I explain, more than a million of us, along with three million Europeans in the UK, will be, according to the British government's own declaration, one of the "main cards" with which they'll gamble in the negotiations.

Perhaps Bettina's got an equally trenchant opinion about that, and if so, I'd like to hear it. Does she think that millions of people are going to be deported from the UK and a million Brits robbed of their security if the government doesn't get what it wants from Brussels? And it won't get what it wants. And where will I be then?

European passports in hand, four million of us switched countries in good faith. Then a few half-demented demagogues persuaded the government to strip us of our privileges. And that, I inform my friend, is a deprivation of rights of residence and equal treatment on a scale not seen since decolonisation. So now we're stranded. And we're terrified!

"Stranded? Terrified?" Bettina cries. "Stop being terrified, get organised and get on with it! Or go to some other school, I don't care. It's not very hard, Tim. Just do the work and learn the language. But for God's sake stop whining."

She pours me another glass and we glare at each other.

...

Back home, I return a missed call to discover that a well-renowned theatre in Watford wants me to direct a production of *Macbeth* in the autumn. Which is wonderful and amazing and great and exciting, but – wouldn't you know it? – the dates clash with the next module. There's a one hundred per cent overlap.

This is what always happens. As a freelancer, obviously I don't control when work comes in, and, when it does, it never fits perfectly around my language learning schedule. What to do? Before the referendum, I'd always take the work. Without any particular rush to master the language, I'd duck out and re-join later. Obviously, though, the referendum has upped the stakes. And yet... I'm making such a balls up of the course. I'm not enjoying school anymore. I've remained largely punctual and attentive, but if I'm honest, my presence has become more like lip service. Though I'm learning new words and understanding new grammar points, and I may even get a pass, I'm not really, properly, meaningfully Learning German.

I enjoyed studying whenever I could fit it in, but since there's been an urgency, I've become to resent it. Call me perverse. The devil inside me resists the whole process of integration if it's to be undertaken on anyone's terms but my own, and especially if the schedule is dictated by the Brexiters.

One of the reasons freelance life appeals to me is that I'm relatively free of bosses. I'm outside the system. As a teenager in the 70s, my gayness forced on me an outsider status, and even now, I'm not a natural joiner. I prefer to find my own solutions to things. Deluded and arrogant though it might sound, I'm tempted to believe that I can find a fix to the problem of how to remain legally and prosperously in Germany without passing exams and going down to the town hall to take a citizenship test.

I talk it through with Sven. On the plus side: directing *Macbeth* is paid work, which I need. I know the play well, and I've always wanted to have a bash at it. With Dad in and out of hospital, it might be good to spend more time in England. I'd have a few months to finish *Emma* before *Macbeth* starts. In fact, a concrete deadline might help polish off the boring old adaptation that my producer requires. It's going to be an exercise in maths. How many characters can I afford? If I'm doubling, what effect will that have on costume changes? It'll be like the British approach to Europe. Costs and logistics. No poetry, no grand ideas, no creativity. No ambition for anything other than earning some money off a popular title.

But what happens to getting the language under my belt? Forget the idea that I can study in the evenings while rehearsing

Macbeth during the day. That never, ever works. But I'm not giving up on learning German forever. Once *Macbeth* is on, I'll return to Berlin and B-1-1 with a different group of students. It's not ideal. The thought of getting to know yet another bunch of bad language learners is daunting, plus a different teacher might be even worse than Almut. Also, without knowing when the guillotine of Article 50 will fall, deferment is potentially a huge risk. I might scupper my chance of citizenship if I take *Macbeth* over German. But work is work.

It seems that tonight's the night for facing facts. Not only has Bettina told me I'm an unlikeable racist, but I also come face to face with yet another unpalatable truth. Painful though it is to admit, taking the job – which I do and gratefully too – shows me precisely where my priorities lie. Evidently, theatre is really a wife to me. So what's Europe then? No better than a mistress? And what of all the little sojourns I've taken, toying with various foreign languages along the way? Nothing but a string of casual affairs I've enjoyed, and then discarded as soon as the mood changed or difficulties emerged.

Friday 1st July

On facetime, Mum tells me the doctors want to move Dad down to Molesey where there's a community hospital. I have no idea what a community hospital is, and am none the wiser after asking. Neither of us wants to use the word 'hospice,' which always sounds like the end, but I fear that's what it is. Perhaps the doctors in Teddington have run out of options. Maybe there's nothing more they can do for him, and it's just a matter of time.

Mum's much more optimistic. The point of the move, she insists, is that in the new place he'll get more attention and have a better physiotherapy regime. She tells me the physio people in Teddington are spectacularly useless, and often don't show up at all. Three weeks ago, he was driving. When he went into hospital a week ago, he could walk ok with a stick, but after seven days of doing practically nothing, he can't get to the loo without a nurse holding him upright.

Despite the fact that it'll mean Mum has further to travel every day, she's relentlessly positive, and only wants to talk about the food she's making and packing into Tupperware boxes and taking with her down to Molesey so he has something nice to eat when he gets there.

...

The sunny uplands of Intermediate beckon everyone but me. Given that I'm putting German on hold, I don't suppose there's much point in my showing up to mark the end of Elementary today. But a potluck's been organised for lunchtime, and I'm dying to see what everyone's brought.

Mira wears a tiny, glittery black cocktail dress and totters around on high heels. Almut asks: film or work. We vote unanimously for work, thus disappointing our teacher who fancied the morning off. She does a bad job disguising her feelings, and Mervyn laughs as if it's the funniest thing he's ever seen. It must be the drugs.

Maybe it's because I'm planning to leave the group that I observe it with more than my customary detachment. Either way, I can't help but marvel this morning at how much my dear classmates are so...themselves.

In my head, Bettina's voice batters at my peace. "You're so superior and grand!"

Even though we elected to study, everyone's sleepy and longing for the holidays. So Almut makes us play a warm-up game. We must work as a team to create a sentence, word by word. We start with Mervyn, who narcissistically chooses the word 'Mervyn'. And off we go around the room.

> **Mervyn:** Mervyn...
> **Felipe:** Mervyn ist...
> **Letizia:** Mervyn ist gestern...
> **Xiu:** (*After much prompting*) Mervyn is gestern am...
> **Me:** (*Brilliantly!*) Mervyn ist gestern am Parkplatz...
> **Karole:** (*Even more brilliantly!*) Mervyn ist gestern am Parkplatz gegangen...

Next is Mira but she rears up like a nervous horse. She's heard the word 'Mervyn' six times in the last minute, not to mention that she and he had a stand-up row only a few days ago, and the pair have spent five days a week locked in a room together since January. But she confesses she has no idea what the word 'Mervyn' means. "That man is Mervyn!" Almut, appalled, points at him with a stiff, angry arm. "Ah," screams Mira, and giggles her barky giggle.

"Hypocrite!" I hear Bettina again, this time reminding me that, if I wish to criticise people for not knowing a name, I should remember that I'm still unsure how to address Xiu after sitting next to her for four weeks.

In fact, no one knows how to address Xiu. Wishing to drag the young woman's attention away from her phone, Almut attempts the old familiar 'Joo', which fails when Xiu ignores her. Rehearsing the usual options, she has a go with 'Shoe', prompting Xiu to look up quizzically. Encouraged, Almut sees a chance to finally nail it. "*'Shoe' ist richtig, oder?*" she asks. ('Shoe' is right, isn't it?') To which Xiu responds with a remarkably placid, "Chew". Finally we know. On the very last day.

Concentration is hard. When I'm not thinking about Dad, his journey down to Molesey and how Mum's coping with the trauma of it all, my mind whirls with ideas about how to stage *Macbeth*. I start to fantasise about the witches. Immediately, Letizia, Milica and Mira present themselves as interesting witch material, with Mervyn as the chief hag, Hecate. I suppose Roberto would be Banquo, the good guy who's constantly being shafted, and Xiu would be a perfect Fleance – says nothing and gets knifed to death in Act Three.

"Murderer!" yells Bettina.

Shit! She's right. Where does this viciousness come from? Apart from doodling and rustling, Xiu hasn't harmed me in the slightest. In fact, she gave me a small smile on arrival today, which, I promise, she's never done before. I was quite shocked. With the spirit of Bettina breathing down my neck, I attempt to see her through fresh eyes.

Even though, on the last day of the course, she chooses to add a white-out pen to her arsenal of plastic stationery, and clicks it incessantly, it's not hard to find pity for her when the group discusses which one of our native tongues has the most cases. After Almut has asked us all in turn, we discover that, with fourteen, Estonian's got the most, English the least, and – yes, you guessed it – Xiu didn't understand the question. But when we talk about the languages we learned at school, she's uncharacteristically chatty, telling us that she was forced to study English, but hated it because exams were always being set and she was never any good. Maybe, one day, she'll do something that really engages her and she'll excel at it. I fervently hope so. Mentally, I wish her well and think how pleased Bettina would be with me.

We revise *als* meaning 'when' – but only sometimes. Unhelpfully, it's 'when' as in 'When I was young' but not 'when' as in 'When is the bus coming?' Almut asks Fairuz, "When were you last happy?" and Fairuz answers: after the birth of her fourth child. She poses the same question to Xiu who responds that she was happy when she found a new host family to live with. This is strange news indeed. Why was she forced to leave her original family? What awful dramas precipitated the departure? What sorrow and suffering can there have been for the usually silent, obedient, unemotional *au pair* to call an end to an unhappy domestic situation, let alone break cover and reveal it to the class? In my head, Bettina urges me to consider the possibility that Xiu's mysterious story might be worth my attention, and that, for four weeks, I've spent breaks talking nonsense with my two most diaphanous classmates, while consistently discounting the only substantial one.

For as long as I've known her, Xiu's been entirely focussed on avoiding communication. But something extraordinary is happening. There's no doubt about it – she's positively expansive today. Here she goes again, raising an arm in order to ask how we sign up for the next module.

Almut slumps into her chair and stares at the ceiling, looking as though she might cry. "I told you already," she says, exasperated. "I gave you the papers to fill in if you want to do B-1-1, and now the deadline's past." Naturally, Xiu didn't understand what the papers meant, and didn't like to ask. Too risky – the expectation of too much loss of face, I suppose. So what's going to happen to her? Without a function in Berlin, will she be recalled to China? Will she have to admit the truth to her backers? Her parents? The

Learning German (badly)

Party? Will she remain in Berlin and go feral – too terrified to face a gruelling debrief back in the Peoples' Republic? Suddenly, an idea occurs to me. I'm already signed up, and I don't need my place. Xiu could take it.

Our textbook ends with renewal. The fictional boss of fictional Maria Torremolinos gives birth. Unknown to the others, Maria drives to the vocabulary-rich senior centre to pick up ancient Aunt Erika so that she can return home and be part of the baby-naming scene. I'm aware that I sound like a mad, spam-faced sap, but I become ridiculously misty eyed about the birth, and everyone's happiness around it, and Maria's kindness in thinking of the old woman, and ancient Aunt Erika's pleasure at being included. I wonder about Dad, and whether he'll ever return from the place where they've put him today.

What is love? Almut looks to us for answers. Karole says, "It's when you know you can trust the other one." It's the second time this morning that she's rolled out an apparently effortless and entirely accurate sentence in German. "Gosh," I gush under my breath, "You've got loads better since last week!" "I know," she agrees, smiling girlishly, and tucking in her chin to regard me through eyelashes, in the faux-humble manner of Princess Diana doing demure.

"What's happened?"

"A week selling handbags!" she whispers.

It's a miracle.

Fairuz's contribution to the 'what is love' question is, "Love is when he gives me money." Tracey, ever the sentimentalist, offers (in English), "Love is when we all come back in the autumn for the next language module." A little flustered, Almut decides for once not to bother steering her back to German, and murmurs through a crooked smile, "Thank you, Tracey". This is the last time I'll sit with these people in this room, so I jettison all inhibitions and declare that, to me, love is when Sven brings me breakfast in bed at the weekend. I could have said a million other things – that love is when he knits me a scarf or darns my sweaters or trims my beard or buys me tulips, or when he hugs me so tight I fear for my circulation, or when we make for the sofa to compare notes about our day and cuddle up under a blanket to listen to each other talk, or when he reaches for my hand in the theatre, or when, from work, he sends me links to interesting things and it occurs to me that I'm on his mind as much as he's on mine. But I say the thing about breakfast in bed because I definitely have all the German words for it. Whether Mervyn's unable to bear the saccharine, or a hangover is kicking in, with a rictus grin, a crimson face and no explanation, he clatters noisily out of the room.

I visit head supremo Frau Fuchs in the school office at break time, persuade her to replace my name with Xiu's on Almut's B-1-1 register and report the news to Xiu who takes ages to understand, but once she does, is pleased. Then I meet up with Karole in the coffee shop. Both startled by Mervyn's red-faced exit, we agree that it must be a drug thing. She's very concerned, and wonders what on earth she ought to do. Alcohol's the bigger issue, she says. Whenever they go out, he invariably gets hammered and makes an idiot of himself. She describes how he becomes boorish and bitchy, and picks fights with strangers. She's seen him thrown out of bars, and even knocked to the ground and strangled. He's a bad drunk. It's as if he enjoys putting himself in danger.

I suggest taking him to AA, but she doesn't seem keen. She's looking for a solution that'll allow her to do more of the rescuing. As if my understanding his history could help Mervyn stop drinking, she relates what she knows of his journey from London to Berlin – how, during his last year in England, the big bucks he was making came at a cost. Apparently, while experiencing increasingly frequent panic attacks, he got to the point where he could only assess peoples' personalities by judging their clothes. It occurred to him that he was losing his mind, and that's when he escaped to Berlin, where he now lives off his savings and grandma's subsidies, fishy and financial.

Learning German (badly)

Although I know a lot about Karole, it occurs to me that I'm ignorant about *her* journey to Berlin. She hardly needs prompting as she recalls the night in a New York cocktail bar when Yannis sauntered in – a handsome European pilot on a stopover. At that point, she and her girlfriends were taking turns to host weekly Botox parties. She knew her life was frantic and suspected it had become a little insane. She was searching for an alternative, and he presented himself as her knight in shining armour. Berlin may be the capital of Europe, but frantic it's not. Here, she owns fewer clothes and fewer things, but she's happier. Having lived all over the world, she wants to remain in one place, and she wants to have a baby. And Berlin will do nicely. Now, it's just a case of persuading Yannis to want the same.

Then I relay to Karole what Tracey once told me – a similar story about living in Dubai with her brothers, raking in the dosh, but feeling lost and miserable, longing to escape her family's overbearing ambitions for her.

Swapping gossip, Karole tells me the Koreans' secret – every night in Seoul, Jang-Mi would drink gin, become violent and break things. They, too, came here to escape self-destructive habits and save themselves.

Milica fled the social conservatism of the Ukraine. Khadra wished to leave behind the corruption and inefficiency of the developing world. "We're all escaping something," I reflect to Karole, who, naturally enough, asks me, "So then, what were you escaping?"

Well, I ponder, if my migration was an escape, and I had to put it into a word, I suppose I was fleeing nationalism. But that feels either too pompous or too ludicrous to admit. I think the truth is that I was actively searching for something, rather than running away from something, and if I had to boil it down to one single thing, it was Europe. I tell her I was looking for Europe.

"Yeah and love," she says, with a cheesy grin. "Same thing," say I.

Mervyn returns at the end of class. We did him a disservice. It wasn't the drugs. To be accurate, it wasn't *only* the drugs. He proudly tells us that, yesterday, he addressed himself to baking something for the end-of-term potluck, and with everyone's dietary limitations in mind, produced a batch of organic, vegan and gluten-free chocolate brownies. This morning, he left them at home, and has returned just in time with a pretty box of non-exclusive, all-embracing goodies. As Mervyn's not famous for his concern for the needs of others, this is extraordinary.

In fact, it turns out that each one of my classmates has considered everyone's dietary requirements. The Koreans juggle hundreds of small plastic pots to offer up a feast of sushi and kimchi and yummy creations called hoeddoek and pajeon and dakjuk. Letizia and Felipe submit homemade humus. Milica's whipped up some vegan chocolate balls. Karole presents a chickpea salad with brown rice that sounds earnest and looks grim, but tastes fabulous. Almut lays a spectacular *Kalter Hund* on the table. Even though she's not able to eat any of it herself, Fairuz has made a lovely almond-based cake for the group to enjoy. I've bought slices of gluten-free *kuchen* from my favourite *Bäckerei*, and Melina contributes a bottle of rosé.

Khadra's away, and with Ramadan ongoing, Leila and Fairuz understandably wish to leave the scene early. But it should not go by without being noted: not only has hefty Fairuz made a cake for us, but she's also pitched up wearing make-up for the first time ever. Rather than her usual forbidding tank of a coat, she's decked out in a huge baggy western-style shirt. It's sea green, dominated by a massive lion's face, horribly gaudy, but miles snazzier than anything we've seen before. And she addresses me. She says, "Tim, you have lost weight." I haven't – but who cares? On the last day, Fairuz and I manage a small conversation. Mental note: I must remember to wear this T-shirt more often.

Leila, on the other hand, is still uninterested in engaging with me. As she and Fairuz leave, I give it one last go, if only to say 'goodbye and happy holidays', but she stares at me as if she'll break into pieces if I utter a word. There's been no headway over four weeks. I'm frustrated with her and ashamed of myself.

Miracle of miracles, Roberto drops by. Fresh from his stay in the squat, he tiggerishly declares his culinary intentions for us all. Francesca might be prevailed on to bring ice cream later. Wait a moment – Francesca is definitely bringing ice cream for everyone later. Hang on there – Francesca is thinking of setting up an ice cream shop over the summer. But you haven't heard anything yet – Francesca and a friend have been investigating how to buy ice on an industrial scale! Who wants what flavour? Let's make a list!

With everyone in receipt of a splash of warmish rosé, class breaks up and we mingle. Roberto tells me about his Köpi experience. The drink, the drugs, the post-punk garage-rock-band that are now his friends – it was all mind-blowing, just what he needed, and, luckily, Francesca's completely cool about the whole temporarily-running-away-from-home thing. In return, I decide to tell him about *Macbeth*. I talk about the ideas I've had overnight.

It took me ages to imagine an adaptation of *Emma* that felt modern while retaining the spirit of the original, but *Macbeth* presents no such problem. In Shakespeare's play, ancient, lawless Scotland feels fantastically post-apocalyptical, and the supernatural element demands a radical solution, so, aiming to synthesise old language with new visuals, I've summoned up a kind of Chechnyan dystopia where, after war with Russia, civilisation has broken down. The witches, who refuse to be bound by time or space, will be female ISIS terrorists and materialise to the wracked warlord holed up in a decaying concrete bunker.

I'm touched that Roberto's so impressed with my concept, but at the same time he's concerned. They'll be moving into the new place in the autumn. Will the job mean I'll miss the flat-warming party? Not to worry. They'll postpone it. For me. All plans will be put on hold until '*il grande Tim*' returns to Berlin. I don't believe a word of it. But I'm touched anyway.

"How's work," I ask Karole.

"I don't want to talk about it." So I dutifully change the subject by asking, "Are you worried about failing?" Karole's taken so many days off, it's technically impossible for her to pass A-2-2.

"Oh, I'm not failing."

"But you were in Greece for four days, and then you missed –" She interrupts. "Almut's passing me, no problem."

"But we're not allowed to miss more than four days. How on earth can you pass?"

"Oh, you know. I had a little chat with her and..." she trails off, shrugging prettily.

"What?" I persist.

"I just explained that it was important for me to pass, and that I'd do better on the next course." She smiles, job done.

In fact, it turns out that everyone except Bled the Albanian passes the module. Even Tracey. Even Xiu. There's general rejoicing, and no one's bothered about Bled. We haven't seen him for weeks.

Soon after we receive our certificates and the Arab ladies depart, a frenzied group conversation ignites about tattoos. If you've got one, you simply *have* to show it. Melina's shyly unsure how to reveal the design on her back with dignity, but, thank heavens, Mervyn's on hand to yank up her shirt for her. Emerging from a delicate soap-bubble inked on her side, a flock of graceful swallows fly up and over an adorable shoulder blade. Less abashed, Roberto clownishly hitches his trousers down to reveal one hip decorated with a grinning, top-hatted, green pony who giddily rears up on its hind legs, and another with a monkey bearing frothing beer and staggering drunkenly about. Mira whispers something to me I can't quite catch, so I give her a confused face and she points at her fanny. The actual tattooed ones keep silently to themselves, eat nothing but their own hummus and leave early.

After tucking my certificate into my rucksack, I slip away and locate my bike among the mountain of bedraggled specimens outside the front of the VHS building. I chuckle to myself when it occurs to me that Francesca failed to turn up with the ice cream. Who's surprised? Roberto, bless him, never provided the address of the place where we should take our electronic stuff for the refugees.

Once home, I add the signed sheet of VHS letter-headed paper to a file of others, and check on Brexit. It's become a reflex action. If there's a pause in the conversation, check to see what's happening in England. Come in from the shops, check to see. Going to bed, better first just check and see.

Facebook's buzzing with news of an anti-Brexit demonstration, organised by a bunch of British ex-pats, and it's happening this evening in Oranienplatz. The Guardian focusses on Gove's leadership bid. That poisonous blancmange of a man addresses the press: "I stand here not as the result of calculation." It's the best joke so far to emerge from the Brexit disaster.

I wonder whether I'll ever see any of my classmates again. I hope Karole will stay in touch, and I'm curious to know what happens to Roberto and Mervyn. To be honest, though class ended an hour ago, it might as well have been a month. I'm already in *Macbeth* mode.

...

It's inconceivable that the authorities anticipated Brexit aggro, but even before we reach Oranienplatz, Sven and I pass at least thirty security vans, green-striped ones and blue-striped ones. In the evening sunshine, small groups of police, all men, stand around the square, bronzed and muscly in their short-sleeved shirts, looking relaxed and chatting among themselves. While a demonstration isn't exactly my kind of thing, Oranienplatz isn't far from home, and I'd go a lot farther to meet people who share my predicament.

Until recently, it was fringed with tents overflowing with North African refugees, but the migrants have been spirited away to better accommodation, and the square has returned to its former use. It's one of Berlin's most popular centres for protest and dissent. By this time of year, the grass is routinely worn away. And when I spot two demonstrations mustering, I understand why the police have turned up. A rally against CETA and TTIP is well attended, blurry in a cloud of dust, and making a hell of a racket.

Much more innocuous-looking, and nervously keeping their distance, is a gaggle of anti-Brexiters attached to a clump of German speakers – one from the left, a green, a federalist and an unwanted nationalist.

By the time we pitch up, it's the federalist who's in full flow, and she's in no mood to feel sorry for the Brits. "Britain has failed to come to terms with its own irrelevance in the new global order," she shouts in immaculate English and with not a little *Schadenfreude*, the gist of her argument being that the UK has only ever seen the European enterprise as a market, an opportunity to bully everyone else, drag its heels over integration and, as the Germans put it, "plead for extra sausage". Her happy conclusion is that since "the English have gone," they won't be around to veto anything, so there can be more pooling of sovereignty, and a serious discussion can finally begin about the creation of a European army, hoorah.

It isn't exactly what the crowd has pitched up to hear. The man next to me tells me he's come in the hope that someone might be able to inform him if his UK qualification will hold good after Brexit. Currently, it allows him to practice as a doctor in Germany, but with two kids in German schools, he's keen to learn if he'll have to leave his job, go back to college and re-qualify. I'm keen to discover if anyone knows whether an EU health insurance card will be defunct after withdrawal.

None of our questions are answered, or could be, but it's inspiriting to be amongst like-minded people for a while, and we proudly add our voice to the crowd's for an hour or so, before heading off to have dinner with Jost and Jochen in the Swiss *Rösti* place round the corner. Too many calories but bloody delicious.

...

On our return, there's a message from Mum saying that Dad had a terrible ambulance journey from Teddington to Molesey. It's only a few miles, but it seemed to take hours. The ambulance was old, he wasn't strapped in properly, and he was rocked about badly. Literally true or not, obviously that's what it felt like to him. She reports that he's been placed in a side-room, and is traumatised and disinclined to eat, let alone walk. He hates the new place, and this evening he was going in and out of actually knowing where he was. The nurses are cheerful and full of talk about tomorrow, but Mum says she's feeling wretched and miserable and alone.

I talk to Sven, and he agrees with me, so I book a flight home. The word 'home' comes instinctively, and tonight, applied to England, seems right.

Saturday 2nd July

I'm flying tomorrow, so it's a day for tying up loose ends. I phone Jana to explain that, regretfully, I'm going to have to pause our tandem sessions for a while. I was looking forward to next week, I tell her. I'd already imagined the discussion we'd have about triggering Article 50, and who has the right to do so. While it's never been an ambition of mine, I seem to be becoming quite the constitutional expert. However, I've hardly begun with news about Dad, when she huskily interrupts with an update of her own. The husband has been out of control all week, doing horrible damage of every kind, and the shit finally hit the fan when her investor-friend made a surprise visit to the apartment, only to receive drunken abuse at the door. Having thus lost all the money, Jana is very sorry, but she can't think about anything else, let alone plan a tandem. She's taken some days off work and has no inclination to move from her bedroom. We speak in English, and she's so distracted that her syntax becomes completely ragged. I figure this isn't the time to correct her.

Remembering my recent row with Bettina, I hide behind an email to her.

...

The Libyans have put up nets! They're utterly ghastly, but a massive improvement on the flag. On one of the windowsills, there's even a pot with a stick of a plant in it. However, it's very much a case of one-step forward and two back when we discover them holding a barbecue in the bike shed. The father has removed half the bikes and is frying chicken. The kids, who we understand are called Momo and Nono, stare at us with expressionless faces as we explain to their Dad that the bike shed is for bikes and the park round the corner is for barbecues. They're perfectly nice people. They don't understand the rules, that's all. We have to keep teaching them and not lose patience.

Certain we've done the right thing, half an hour later Sven and I are riven with doubt. It was just a barbecue. They'd probably have replaced the bikes once they'd finished. What have we done? We didn't even mention how nice their curtains looked. We're monsters.

We spend the evening on the terrace with the perky snapdragons, the straggly cosmos and our wonderfully loopy desert plants. I try to bring Sven up to speed with Brexit news, but he'd rather our last evening in goodness-knows-how-long wasn't all about bloody politics. He's convinced that sustaining my current level of anxiety is threatening my sanity. Maybe his too.

But, as he unscrews a bottle of wine, I won't be silenced, and I yatter on with all the latest from the Tory leadership race, which currently looks like a straight fight between Theresa May and an under-whisked, over-baked version of Theresa May called Andrea Leadsom. She's a banker whom no one's ever heard of, and is said to be a sort of British Le Pen but without the talent. Therefore, everyone's willing May to win, despite the fact that her claim to the role of leading a Brexiting government is that she spent the last three months campaigning for Remain.

I want to talk money, but Sven makes a toast and refuses to take me seriously. Whether he wants to hear it or not, the facts are grim. Sterling's fall means that my already limited financial clout has effectively been reduced by about twenty per cent in a week. The whole thing's making me ill, and my eczema's got worse.

"Everything will be alright in the end," he assures me.

Everything will be alright?! How's he so certain? He doesn't read the papers. The man knows nothing.

"What happens if the planes won't fly come Brexit day?"

"Oh, they'll work something out."

"But the country's going to have to revert to 1970s food standards."

"Nobody will die if they can't eat blueberries all year round. England needs a reality check, anyway."

"Ok, forget about politics. What about us?"

"What *about* us?"

"Well, what do you think will happen if I get ill? One of those illnesses that means I'm in and out of hospital for weeks, or months, or even years? We're not young. It might happen."

"We'll cope," he says.

"So are you going to pay for me to get treated in a German hospital?" I ask, "Because after Brexit, I won't be insured. Which means I'll have to get help in England. And we don't have anywhere to live in England. We don't *want* to live in England."

"Then we'll get you medical insurance here," he says.

"We can't afford it."

"We'll find a way," he reassures me.

"Ok, then, what happens if Dad dies and I need to spend time with Mum and I get ill in England? If I'm insured here, I'll lose my access to the NHS. What then? And what happens when you retire, and we want to move to, say, Portugal. You can, and I can't."

"Course you can," he says. "Are we moving to Portugal then?"

"Are you guaranteeing I'll be entitled to my UK state pension in Portugal?"

Sven's got a reassuring answer for everything, though it's all wishful thinking.

Still, he's right about one thing. If a crisis emerges, we'll tackle it. As long as we're together, stuff works out ok. And, aware that tomorrow we'll be apart, I eventually wind in my unquenchable anxiety and do a good job of pretending none of my concerns are real. By the third glass, I appear to have accepted that Brexit's the future. The evening's warm, and the flowers are glorious, and my gorgeous lover is beautiful and funny, and I love him most when he gets tripped up by an English idiom. Brexit isn't going to be 'the straw that breaks the camel's neck', he says. I remember asking him once whether there was a German version of 'mutton dressed as lamb', and he thought a bit, and answered with another question, "Does that mean the same as 'a wolf in cheap clothing'?" And when he says 'layouted' instead or 'laid out', or 'sore in the eye' instead of 'eyesore'. or 'fuzzy water' instead of 'fizzy water', or when he pluralises 'information' to 'informations' or 'advice' to 'advices' or 'hair' to 'hairs' ("Yes, they're very long, I must have them cut"), then I know that somehow, somewhere, we'll find a way to stay together, being happy forever.

He dribbles the remainder of the bottle into my glass and, in the blue light, the white flowers glow, and his English starts to break down. He forgets basic constructions and his accent sounds stranger and sweeter. And when he pronounces words that have a 'y' at the end, like 'easily' and 'Germany' and 'probably', he elongates the 'eee', making me burble with pleasure, and it's easy to imagine that, whatever happens in England or Germany, everything will, indeed, be alright in the end.

But several hours later, a dream wakes me up. I'm breathless and sweating.

"Wha'?" asks Sven, not fully conscious.

In my head, a hundred barrels, all on fire, are tumbling down a hill towards me, each one an unanswerable question. It's that dream again, the one where the questions multiply into myriad others and I can't distinguish what the real question is. And I won't know what it is until they sort Brexit out and tell me where I stand.

The summer in London

We can now add lungs to the list of major organs that are failing. Is skin a major organ? If so, put that down as well. Dad's psoriasis is out of control. His bedsores are extraordinary. In terms of his pills, they can't achieve the right balance and, as a result, he's suffering from extreme water retention. And yet he insists he'd be better off at home. So we try and keep him calm and tell him the doctors need him to stay here in hospital for a little bit longer.

A couple of days later, he stops eating. To me, it's obvious that he's decided to call it a day, but Mum clings to the idea that it must be to do with (another new problem) his difficulty in swallowing. A team of physios who specialise in the jaw are called. They even wheel him downstairs for an MRI to see whether he's suffered brain damage, and if so, whether it's caused some kind of change in the way his tongue works. But you just have to look at it to understand. It's hard and shrivelled, somewhere between mauve and black.

It's amazing that the doctors won't discuss the fact that he's dying. They're convinced they can cure him. Or they pretend to be. The senior doctors tell the lie with more panache, while the juniors struggle. Responding to the need for good news in our eyes, they nearly give the game away. According to the man that makes the decisions, a slight adjustment in the treatment will return the patient to his old self in the wink of an eye – just like he was, with all his old powers back, with no cost and hardly any effort. The guy's obviously fulfilling an agenda we're not party to. In this system, there can be no credence given to the idea that the old must pass away.

One day my father's talking, the next he isn't. One day he's gentle and sweet, thinks he's at home and suggests we all go into the garden. The next, he's angry, ranting and accusing everyone of trying to kill him. Mum spends each morning making a variety of nutritious milky things, and then, in the afternoons, tries to tempt him to eat at least one of them.

Back in Teddington Hospital, he's put into a room with a faded picture of a pair of owls on the wall. The paintwork's cracked, the curtains don't work, one of the windows won't close. Half the nurses are considerate and hardworking, the other half might as well not bother showing up. When hypothermia is diagnosed, he's moved again, this time to a ward where a man to one side of him continually shouts and a guy on the other side cries. Dad announces to anyone who'll listen that he's had enough and wants to go. But a nurse called Ron produces a large transparent, plastic lilo-type thing to put on top of him to keep him warm, and connects it to a machine that pumps in hot air. Outside, the sun is baking the trees, so, despite his plummeting internal temperature, he doesn't feel particularly cold. He hates the new device and spends all his conscious time trying to push it off.

In the face of all this, Mum is still behaving as if he's going to make it. We have a chat in the hospital cafeteria, during which I suggest it might be helpful if she let Dad know that she accepts that he's leaving us. He's told us he wants to go, so we should let him go. And, bravely, reluctantly, Mum edges a little way towards agreeing.

After a couple more days, he isn't talking at all, and his breathing worsens. His lungs are flooding with fluid and when pneumonia is diagnosed, Sven books a flight over.

We're all with him when, mid-afternoon two days later, he takes his last painful, gravelly, water-clogged breath.

There are practical things to keep me busy. They help me avoid feeling anything but numb. We're taken to a little side-room where kind nurse Dolores from Spain gives Mum a cup of tea. She wants me to accept an NHS leaflet about what to do next, and in what order: register the death, arrange the funeral and so on. I go to store it in Mum's handbag for safekeeping, only to discover that it's full of pegs. She was determined to get the washing in before we left for the hospital.

The staff is kind but busy, so it's time for us to go. There's a flurry of indecision about what we should leave and what we should bring away with us. I return to Dad's bed, now tactfully surrounded by curtains, though the noisy guy's still shouting. Deciding to leave his sticks to the hospital, I collect a sponge bag, the pair of hearing aids he'd stopped wearing a couple of weeks ago, and his spectacles, but his razor is nowhere in sight. With the aid of a nurse, we turn everything out of the little bedside cabinet, placing the contents on the bed, carefully avoiding the body, until eventually, the hunt for the razor seems an absurd step too far. Whether I find it or not, we're still losing Dad. I abandon the hunt. Turning for the last time to my father, I say goodbye.

Now we have to walk away, walk out of the ward, find the car park and get Mum home.

Once there, one of the first things she asks me to do is dismantle the giant jigsaw puzzle they'd been working on for upwards of half a year – a view of the Alps in summer, absurdly prettified meadows and fairy tale huts. On completion, they realised that a single but central piece was missing. Alina the cleaner was detailed to rummage round the skirting boards, though no doubt Dad had dropped it and Alina herself had inadvertently hoovered it up months ago. The all-but-completed puzzle has been kept out on display, hogging the dining room table because Dad wanted his friend Ken to come over and see it. But Dad was constantly a bit under the weather, and when he was feeling alright, old Ken wasn't so great, so the visit never happened.

I ask Sven to help me pack it away. The thing hardly breaks at all. We manage to fold it up with only a few pieces sticking out like broken bones. I place it in the box and push down the lid, which provides stiff resistance against the noisy air rushing out, and I hear one of Dad's last breaths, wheezy and effortful.

The next day, I hide behind logistics and paper work, closing accounts, unsubscribing Dad from memberships, retitling things, registering, arranging, calling his friends and talking on the phone to cousins I haven't spoken to in decades. As old as me, they sound like a memory I have of their parents, my largely dead aunts and uncles. At first my throat clenches and my eyes fill with tears, and once or twice I'm rendered speechless. But the next day, when I have to report to the banks and the insurance companies, "My father died a couple of days ago," it's easier. I feel guilt. Even a day diminishes the impact. Time moves us on, and we leave Dad behind. He can't come with us tomorrow and the day after, and I imagine our memory of him weakening, however hard we try to retain it, by the day, by the week, by the month, by the year.

The hardest job turns out not to be a phone call, but an email to the institute, the professional body that he belonged to through work. While I'm sure he'd be thrilled that the service plan for the Ford Focus is now someone else's responsibility, I imagine he'd be devastated to witness me terminate his link to the organisation to which he belonged throughout his entire career, especially after struggling so hard to join, qualifying via night-school five evenings a week, working eighteen hour days when my brother and I were little. Proud of my own theatre work, I relate to his professional pride, and I can barely see the keyboard as I type, "I regret to inform you that..."

On the third day, Sven has to return to work. After driving him to Gatwick, Mum and I spend the evening watching 'Finding Nemo' on DVD. Then, after we've said goodnight to each other, she suddenly blurts out, "Oh, I can't bear to think about where he is." For a moment I don't know what she means. And then I see Dad in bed in the ward with the shouty man, when I couldn't find the razor, lying motionless, as pale as soap. But that's not what Mum means. She sees him where he must surely be now, in the cold white mortuary in the basement of the hospital, waiting to be transported, as soon as I get the paper work organised, to a funeral home in Kingston. She imagines him there – as if alive – alone, and wondering why we've abandoned him.

Aware we had to leave the hospital, I clutched his sponge bag and we turned our backs. Navigating the corridors, we felt like we were floating, walking in slow motion. We found the car in the car park, and we drove away. We felt weird and lost, but we didn't feel, like I do now, that we were disloyal cowards fleeing the battle, abandoning one of our own kind behind enemy lines.

...

We grieve for Dad, but we know that, looked at cosmically, one man's life is only a footnote within a footnote of a larger history. Similarly, Brexit is a footnote within a footnote to the history of the inevitable evolutionary journey that ends with continental union. In the grand scheme of things, it's just a bit of a political misstep. And the civil war raging within both main parties is just a barnacle on the footnote to that.

Separation and disconnection are nothing new. Europe has been split by plenty of tectonic-scale spasms before now. Politically and culturally at odds with itself – east against west, north against south, Germanic against Slavic, and Latinate against both – the Great Schism of 1056 was only the first of multiple fault lines exposed during the enterprise of keeping Europe in one piece. The Roman Empire split into a western and an eastern segment. Then Rome broke from Byzantium, Catholicism from Orthodoxy, Protestantism from Catholicism, the Empire from the Papacy. In 2016, Britain loosens its ties to the mainland. The earth's mantle keeps shifting.

Fearing a further rift – possibly called Nexit, Swexit or Frexit – European leaders gather on the island of Ventotene off the coast of Naples to call for a "new impulse" that will strengthen the current integrationist project.

Learning German (badly)

The place is well-chosen. It was on Ventotene in 1941 that one of my heroes, Altiero Spinelli, spirited into being a document that helped set Europe back on its federalist path during one of its greatest disruptions. Imprisoned by Mussolini, the antifascist scribbled his manifesto onto sheets of cigarette paper, which he hid in a tin box and arranged to have smuggled out of the camp. His ideas circulated among the Italian resistance, eventually achieving acclaim, and inspiring Monnet and Schuman to introduce the supranational institutions that would, in the future, allow Europe to solve its problems through cooperation, rather than serial and evermore deadly conflict.

Together, national leaders Renzi, Merkel and Hollande pay their respects at Spinelli's tomb.

From pathos to bathos. The world reacts with amusement and horror to the news that Boris Johnson – sexist, racist and compulsive liar – a man who once said that a Muslim woman wearing a burka resembles a bank robber – is given the job of Foreign Secretary. By inviting him to represent British diplomacy, newly-elected PM Theresa May 'kills two flies with the same swat', as the Germans would say, insulting anyone who isn't a Conservative Party member and reducing the country to a bad joke. Well, if she wants to play party politics with Europe, it'll destroy her, just as it destroyed her three predecessors.

Hardly less bizarre is David Davis's promotion to the newly-invented role of Brexit Secretary. This is a man who doesn't know that the EU shares a land border with the UK, because he thinks 'Southern Ireland', as he calls it, is part of Britain. He also believes he can negotiate with each of the EU member states individually. (The truth is they only negotiate as a bloc.) He expects that, even after border controls are imposed, the remaining twenty-seven EU members will allow the UK tariff-free access to the single market. (They won't.) He's certain that Britain can immediately start work on securing new trade deals with other countries. (It can't.) And he estimates that it will only take one or, at the most, two years to agree terms. (Britain's never agreed a trade deal with anybody in less than four.)

Up-jerking a middle finger to Brexit, heads of German industry declare their loyalty to the single market, while Paris and Frankfurt ready themselves to welcome international banks when they relocate from London. Dire warnings from industry, science and the arts compete for attention. A loss of subsidies threatens the very fabric of rural life. There's talk that the UK will have to pay a kind of 'divorce bill' that could run into tens of billions of pounds. On the plus side, there are rumours of a new Brexit 50p piece! We're going to get our blue passports back (though they'll be printed in France)! Farage is banging on about an additional bank holiday to celebrate his Independence Day!

Most MPs voted Remain, and privately, they remain Remainers. Publicly, though, they fall over themselves to support a restriction on the free movement of people, or they stay silent on the subject. Opinion shapers become Brexiters even if they're not. The country resembles a political rally in Stalinist Russia where, for fear they'll identify themselves as freethinkers, no one dares to be the first to stop clapping. Freethinkers are called on in the night and taken off to the gulags. Everyone keeps on clapping.

The long and glorious British tradition of keeping the greatest number of people in the greatest amount of ignorance rolls triumphantly on. Remain MPs in Leave constituencies would rather betray their beliefs than explain them. Fearing deselection, they're reluctant to reveal to their constituents the extent to which they were lied to, or inform them that they'll be the ones to suffer the most from Brexit.

Brexiter diehards like Gove and Johnson dismiss doubt as defeatism. Their vision for the UK's future is a neoliberal fantasy island with fewer employment regulations and lower wages – an offshore paradise for Russian, Chinese and Nigerian money. But if England becomes a kind of Singapore-on-Thames, what sort of deals will it secure with partners who know it's desperate?

When will it realise that its precious, newly-regained sovereignty isn't worth anything; that turning its back on federal integration will only reveal that the opposite of integration is disintegration; that political freedom from the EU has been won at the price of political isolation in a merging world?

But "the will of the people must be respected!!"

Facing May and her loyal Leaver lackeys is Michel Barnier, Head of the EU's Brexit taskforce. He was taught in the French civil service, where they train you, like diplomatic Special Forces, to search out and ruthlessly attack the weaknesses of your adversary. But in this case, the adversary poses little threat and is spectacularly unready. The proud new Brexiting departments don't have the manpower, and they don't know which questions to pose, let alone what answers to hope for. Theresa May's gone on holiday without leaving a note about whether she wants the UK to remain in the Single Market or not. It's going to be the Congress of Vienna all over again, with Barnier as Prince Metternich running rings round the arrogant, ill-prepared little Englanders.

...

Sven returns from Germany for the funeral. Everything's been pretty well organised, so we only have to get our suits on and wait for the cars. There's lots of milling about in the kitchen and the hall. We can't believe how smart we all look. We go through the eulogies one last time. Mine's overrunning.

Mum draws the curtains in the front room, not only to keep the sun off the Parker Knolls, but also because it seems the right thing to do on the day you cremate your husband – a sign, I suppose, to the rest of the street. She looks small and vulnerable as she wrestles the heavy, lined curtains, and makes a poor job of it. Through a gap, I spot her friend from across the road, Pam, emerge from her house and head for her car.

I've spent much of the last couple of weeks helping to organise today's events, but I finally get it: this is not just our loss. The point is that it's a communal thing. And with that realisation, I'm moved by the thought that everyone's making such big efforts, taking time away from their lives and descending *en masse* on Teddington. I have serious concerns about holding it together during my speech.

Then the cars arrive. There are two, the lead one bearing the coffin, the other for us. They're early, so they sit in the middle of the road blocking the traffic and waiting. "Cars are here," I announce to the house.

There was a choice – should the hearse come here or should we meet it at the crematorium? Mum wanted it to be driven to the house. "He must come home one last time," she said. Stick in hand, handbag hanging from her shoulder, she hobbles into the front room to look through the gap in the curtains to make sure Dad's there, ready and waiting for us. Perhaps her thinking is that if he leads us to the crematorium, then it'll be less unbearable, for us and for him. That was his job, after all. Leading us.

On arrival at the chapel, they're playing the 'Sanctus' from Fauré's Requiem. It's no surprise. We chose it. You can have whatever you want played by whomever you want. The computer's got everything. Celebrant Cynthia merely has to press the appropriate button. But how the hell did we expect Fauré's 'Sanctus' to help us at all? There's no way I'm getting through this damned eulogy in one piece.

But I do. Kind of. Well enough, anyway. I talk about what Dad achieved at work and in his family life, and I make it clear that, to me, among his greatest virtues was his honesty, his integrity and the fact that he was someone you could trust with your life.

I suppose we're all men of our time. In the new world of Brexit, the values my father cherished and lived by seem suddenly redundant and quaintly old-fashioned. Honesty? Brexit is a lie and was sold with lies. It frightens me to think how a younger generation will prosper when the Brexiting government is so cavalier about abandoning the convictions my father lived by and, through example, imbued in me.

Once we're at the wake, Cynthia tells me that she's been made a grandmother. When the service was over, she checked her messages and read that while she was officiating Dad's cremation, her daughter gave birth to a daughter of her own. She excuses herself so she can drive into Kingston to be with the new mum.

"I want to be there for her", she says.

There for her! That's it! That's what I should have said in my eulogy! Anyone who knew Dad could have talked about his honesty and his integrity, but, as his oldest son, I was in a unique position to talk about his 'there-ness'.

Quietly but consistently, he was there for me when I was young, and he didn't flinch from being there for me when I came out as both gay and theatrical, neither of which he would have chosen for me, had it been up to him. He and I went through at least three complicated decades when we hardly saw eye to eye – but he never turned away from me. He wasn't one to make a fuss or do loads of talking. I did not get my dramatic flair from him. Still, he managed to be steadily and consistently there, unobtrusively but unshakeably.

How lucky I've been. He lived to such an age that we had a chance to work everything out, and had plenty of post-schism years to enjoy each other. There's neither rancour nor resentment – no unresolved issues that need a therapist's attention. As before, he's there for me, but this time as an entirely benign memory. And for that I am truly grateful.

That's what I should have said.

Autumn

Back in Berlin, the weather becomes shifty. It feels summery as long as the sun dominates the shortening days, but, then, suddenly there's a touch of mist and a chill in the air, and we turn on the heating. Sunflowers wobble drunkenly in improvised street gardens, and the chestnut trees that shade our courtyard turn orange. Under them, sleek and shiny conkers dot the tarmac by the bike shed. Our terrace plants become blowsy, with wild, tangled stems.

The news from Westminster is that uncertainly is the new normal. Months on from referendum day, British TV comedians once again provoke easy laughter by including the words 'Europe' and 'boring' in the same sentence. Instead of working to find consensus and solutions, the government is into xenophobia, mendacity and threats.

PM May and I went to the same university and studied the same subject within a year of each other, but while I emerged from Oxford with the notion that cosmopolitanism is the glory of our age, she appears to have picked up the idea that it's a kind of criminal fraud.

At her party conference in Birmingham, she declares that "If you believe you're a citizen of the world, you're a citizen of nowhere". German anti-Semitic discourse saw the 'rootless Jew' as a 'cosmopolitan' citizen from 'nowhere' – an idea that was used to justify the Final Solution. Stalin also called Jewish intellectuals 'rootless cosmopolitans' shortly before he purged them. With the racists in Britain walking tall since June 24th, the PM signals to the world that 1930s-style fascist ideas live at the heart of her government.

Learning German (badly)

...

Since the end of our module together, I've heard nothing from Karole but that she remains under-remunerated, overworked and aggrieved by every aspect of the handbag shop. They're not paying her correctly or on time, while simultaneously insisting she puts in more than the agreed hours.

Then a message arrives from her inviting me for a cuppa and, very much as a P.S., as if she's now bored by the whole subject, letting me know that she's successfully had 'certain stipulations' inserted into her contract, namely that she need no more do overtime or work on Sundays, and that they'll now give her decent breaks and pay her promptly for the hours she puts in. Typically, she omits to explain how these ameliorations have been achieved.

I'm unsurprised. This is a woman who could simultaneously hold a party with and without alcohol, persuade Almut to give her a 'pass' when she hadn't attended nearly enough classes, join a health scheme *before* she got a job, and, by the beginning of July, confidently speak German despite the fact that she was one of the least promising students throughout the previous month. This magnificent creature makes her own luck and does whatever she wants. No doubt, she'll be married and pregnant before Christmas.

Less lucky is Jana, my German tandem partner. While I was staying with Mum in Teddington, none of my emails generated any response from her. On my return, I find out that she's in Calabria for a three-week vacation – with the kids but without the husband. Even after she's due back, she remains uncommunicative, and I imagine her plagued with the usual Jana-type catastrophes. After my fourth call goes unreturned, I go round to make sure she's in one piece. But no one stirs.

Then, out of the blue, an email arrives suggesting a meeting, which I heartily agree to, and by the time I arrive at her apartment,

I'm prepared with a hundred questions about health insurance and dual citizenship so that she can help me practise them in German.

I've had a change of heart. I admit I cannot independently move around the German system. There is no way to live safely and surely in Berlin that doesn't involve playing by the rules. Having said that, I've come to the radical conclusion that I don't any more want to be German. When Brexit threatened, I craved it very much, but more recently I've realised I don't. If I wanted to become German I'd have worked harder and learned the language. It's not beyond Tracey or Xiu, so it's not beyond me. The exam isn't even very difficult. The questions are the same every year. You can look at old tests; they're all available. But I'm not German and I never will be.

There's a TV show that airs on a Sunday evening. It's a cops and robbers procedural, and you can't really consider yourself to be *ein echter Deutscher* if watching it isn't part of your weekly routine. It's taken me four years to be able to say it: I don't like it. In the theatre, I will never accept that a subsidised twelve-week rehearsal period is better for preparing a production than an unsubsidised three. My thinking, manner, humour and anarchic laziness mark me out as English, and those things aren't ever going to change.

What I am and what I want to remain is European, to be able to live in and travel around the continent whenever, however and for as long as I want, like a Roman citizen in Hadrian's days. And if getting German citizenship is the means to that end, then I will reluctantly go through with it. I will practise with Jana how to ask a lawyer what paperwork I need to apply for my rights, how to ask the officer at the town hall to book me in for a language test, and how to talk to companies about medical insurance. But I won't ever be German.

With horror, I realise that I sound exactly like a Brexiter. I can't be arsed to learn the language. I don't want to get involved or accept anything that isn't what I already know, but I would like all the benefits that being European could afford me. I am horrified by myself. If I'm anything to go by, the European project is doomed.

In my head, though, I feel more European than ever. Having a fling at learning German reminds me that all European nations are merely branches of the same tree. In reading *Macbeth*, I hear Plutarch and Petrarch and ask myself how anyone who writes in English can believe his language or his culture stops at the English Channel? Nearly all my British heroes are Europeans. Wilde, Beckett, Joyce, Shaw and Stoppard arrived as foreigners and ended up reinventing the language to tell us who we are. Linguistically, we're European mongrels. Culturally, we're all Made in Greece.

For me, this is both undeniable and a source of immense pride. Federation isn't uniformity. That's the point. We are different. But united. The decision about whether to become a German citizen, or into which state's health system to pay, is just so much logistical detail. Whichever passport I'm allowed to carry, spiritually I'll always be a European.

So as I ring Jana's doorbell I am ready to talk logistics, but she leads me to the kitchen while initiating a breathless monologue about what's been happening to her.

Not only is she divorcing her husband, but she's also abandoning her job without another lined up. After years of fearfully clinging to miserable work, she's kicking over the traces to see what happens if she's brave. This is incredible, wonderful tidings.

And there's more. She's given notice to her landlord to vacate, while the soon-to-be-ex-husband has decided his life would be improved by taking up residence on the couch of a heavy-drinking friend. So next month, she and her kids are moving. Apparently, the trigger was when someone mentioned that New Zealand's a land of endless possibilities and one in which a kids' cookery school would be just the thing to prove successful. Based on that little sliver of undigested hearsay, she's migrating there!

She regrets that our sessions will have to end, but she hopes I'll be pleased for her. If nothing else, as soon as she relocates to a country with few Germans in it, her English will improve leaps and bounds. Oh, and would I like to have a look at the books she's leaving behind, and take some with me? Would I do her a favour and choose some of the CDs she can't be bothered to ship? Could I use a large jam-making pot or a pair of scales? How about a brand new Swiss ball complete with pump? And look, here's a scrapbook that Lilly's classmates have made for her to show that they'll miss her and to wish her well in her new life on the other side of the planet.

I abandon all hope of discussing citizenship. The evening's about her, and her dreams of a more rewarding and peaceful life in another country. As she and I leaf through Lilly's scrapbook together, she handles it almost reverentially.

She becomes reflective. The thing's packed full of hearts and rainbows and badly rendered kiwis fondly sketched by the girl's eight-year-old friends, one page per classmate. Seemingly transfixed by each image, she explains to me who every class member is, their name, what they're like, and the ins and outs of their relationship with Lilly.

Looking up at me a bit shell-shocked, she confides that she's worried that the kids might find it tricky adjusting to a new place.

How to respond? I tell her what Sven tells me. "Everything will be alright," I say.

...

While my erstwhile classmates begin B-1-1, circling ever closer to the prized target of citizenship, I fly to England to start rehearsals for *Macbeth*. I'm delighted to report that both Macbeth and Lady Macbeth seem unequivocally lovely, and I can't wait to spend four weeks shut up in a rehearsal room with them. The company adores my ideas about the post-apocalyptic Chechnyan setting, and each witch is hungrier than the next to explore what it is to be an ISIS terrorist. Unfortunately, when we start technical rehearsals, and the hags are first seen around the building touting AK45s in full niqab and bomb vests, the Front of House Manager is convinced that Watford is under attack. He phones the police, and the building is cordoned off for three hours. Traumatised and in fear of complaints from the public, the theatre's board refuses to grant us permission to pursue the concept, and I'm forced to come up with a 'more traditional' approach overnight. Do you suppose that Ostermeier would ever encounter such philistinism?

...

On a sunny Tuesday morning before work one day, Sven and I cycle over to the Standesamt (the townhall) on Parochialstrasse in Mitte, and, at the appointed time, meet up with Bettina on the steps outside. As you can imagine, the process of getting married is rather longwinded. There's lots of formality and bureaucracy involved. For example, we've had to make this appointment in order to make yet another appointment to actually get civil partnered. That's what you must do. And Bettina is necessary because, my German being what it is, I'm required to have a translator in tow.

In an office whose walls are decorated with photos of Floridian manatees, we present the obligatory paperwork – reams of it – all expensively translated so everything's in both languages – and, to our delight and immense relief, the *Standesamtin* (townhall officer), the delightful Frau Zätzsch, declares that everything's in order. So what date would we like? Having rehearsed the answer, we request November 14th – the fifth anniversary of our very first meeting. Unnecessarily, we also explain what it means to us, and how we love the symmetry. After consulting the calendar, she shakes her head. November 14th is a Monday, and – haven't we read the stipulations? – Berlin doesn't do civil partnerships on Mondays. But look, she says, a twinkle in her eye, everything's approved and stamped. We have a translator with us. We need no more. Why not do it now? Save coming back again.

Shocked, Sven and I regard each other. According to the rules, this is a profoundly unique offer for a townhall officer to make. Suddenly we're the ones dragging our heels. It certainly wouldn't be what we'd planned. I'm wearing my second-hand ripped jeans, and he's got on a thirty-year-old T-shirt, on which there's a purple monkey pointing a gun and saying, 'Kiss, Kiss, Bang, Bang.'

He smiles at me. "But why not?" he asks. And in that moment, I can't think of a single reason to delay. So surrounded by giant aquatic beasts, questions are asked and answered, implications listed, assurances made and last chances passed. Almost before we know it, even before half-past-nine in the morning, we're married in the eyes of God and Frau Zätzsch, and a teary Bettina.

We take ourselves off to a little bar by the Spree and sit with a bottle of *Sekt*, all flushed and breathless and euphoric in the bright congratulatory sunshine, and make a first stab at planning bi-national wedding celebrations.

For all our friends, this is going to be a big surprise, but my thoughts quickly turn to Dad. The most common way he enters my head these days is via things I do or see or learn that I want to share with him. 'Oh, I must remember to tell Dad' is swiftly confounded with the realisation that I can't. These small, sharp regrets seem to be the method by which I'm finally to get used to the loss. I don't have to accept it, but I must get used to it.

There's death and there's renewal.

I like being married more and more. I never thought it would make any difference to the way I feel about Sven or our relationship. The impulse to marry was more to do with the rights it would confer on us, about fabulously dry subjects such as inheritance. But I discover the legal advantages are at least matched by an increase in emotional security. Taking Sven for granted sounds negative, but marriage turns it into an art form. Trust was never lacking, but there's even more of it now. I never thought there could be greater intimacy between us, but there is. Things were never difficult, but they've become even smoother.

I am not England and Germany's not Europe. I can't solve my country's relationship with the continent. But I love my relationship with Sven and I plan to continue to enjoy it, work on it, sustain it and nurture it. In terms of my contribution to European brotherhood, that, after all, is as far as I can go.

Winter

2016 has witnessed the best-produced Eurovision Song Contest ever, but, on all other fronts, it's been a bastard of a year. Not only has my dear old father died, but so too has Victoria Wood and David Bowie. First we have Brexit, and, a few months later, Trump gets the Republican Nomination. What the hell else can possibly go wrong?

Wait. What?

Really?!

But, sadly, it's no joke. After racism's wins in the UK, white supremacy triumphs in America. On the same night Donald Trump is elected President, in Germany a neo-Nazi group is emboldened to celebrate the anniversary of an event that happened, to the day, seventy-eight years earlier: *Kristallnacht*. The group posts a map of Jewish-owned Berlin businesses on Facebook, entitled 'Jews Among Us'. At first, there's a refusal to take it down. But a concerted chorus of disapproval in the German Parliament and press wins the day, and Facebook finally concedes, agreeing to remove it.

In Britain, the governing class knows Brexit is suicidal, but both main parties lack a coherent and credible leader. There's no vision at the top, and the voices of sanity remain cowed and mute. Electoral irregularities, so egregious that if the referendum had been binding the result would have disqualified, come to light. Where's the party leader who's willing to name and confront the erosion of democracy's fundamentals? When High Court judges rule against the Executive by announcing that parliamentary approval is needed to trigger Article 50, the Daily Mail condemns them as 'enemies of the people' and demands that May 'crush the saboteurs'. The backlash against the lawmakers is febrile and furious, but the government does nothing to restrain it. Reading the papers in Germany, it seems that in

England a sort of mob psyche has swelled to fill the power vacuum.

The England I know is dead.

...

My father's passing was the opposite of surprising. The end didn't feel like a sea change, but more the natural termination of a good and long life. But the mark it's making on me is finally dawning. Talk about the end of an era. I had a troubled relationship with both Dad and my country, and it's disorienting, to say the least, to have the pair of them vanish at the same time. I can only assume the coincidence is God's little joke. I've spent the last few months grieving for a place that no longer exists, for people who are no longer there and for possibilities that are no longer open.

Practised at visiting the Teddington twosome, I now go to see Mum and a photo of Dad. It's not enough – no more than whatever kind of Brexit is finally agreed on will be enough.

In the weeks after he went, friends would test my emotional condition, and I would find myself talking about how my mother was taking it all. Suddenly thrust into the position of the oldest man in the family, I accepted new responsibilities. I didn't think about it, I simply performed them, happily, even eagerly. It was the strangest thing to find myself suddenly compliant and helpful: a new me.

Of course, for Mum, nothing could replace Dad. However efficiently I picked up the office duties, I couldn't fill the void that materialised in her life after more than sixty years of partnership with the same man. But I did whatever I could. And, fully occupied by paper work, there was little time for reflection. Sometimes I feared that I felt nothing at all. People would ask, 'How are you doing?' and I would say, "Well, I think it was a terrific shock for Sven...". Or I would chat about Mum's reaction and how brave she was being, and how sorry I felt for her, without ever thinking of talking about myself. After all, her loss was on a whole other scale from mine.

But eventually the admin got done, and I found myself rocketing from one extreme to the other. I became resentful if people didn't ask me how I was coping. I'd immediately turn a conversation so I could present my homily on the subject of my father. At one particular brunch, five different people asked me "how I was feeling?" and I delivered to each a lengthy and identical anguish-stricken monologue, by the end of which I was profoundly knackered. No doubt, it was a necessary catharsis. I've never felt the need to do it again.

I think I'm edging towards some kind of balance, and it arrives accompanied by further realisations. I'm brought face to face with the less than pleasant awareness that I'm next for the chop myself. Of course, one knows one's mortal, but now I really *get* it. Now I occasionally notice my skin, the way it wrinkles on my arm where it never did before. I'm seeing my grandmother's arm.

The past half a year has changed me irrevocably. Sven and I agree that acceptance of our new situation is good. But we're also aware that we must consciously raise our eyes from the ground, develop fresh ambitions and explore new projects, or risk slipping too comfortably into playing a pair of peevish old grouches, sitting snugly on the sofa conversing exclusively about our fascinating illnesses and the death of friends.

Likewise, eventually I suppose I'll have to make some kind of accommodation with Brexit. Accommodation, maybe. Acceptance, never. You won't hear me agreeing that we have a duty to bear the referendum result and find the least bad way to implement it. Whether I am, personally, a lousy embodiment of European integration or not, I'll always be a passionate political advocate for a united, federal, peaceful and prosperous Europe of which Britain is a member.

Learning German (badly)

...

A jolly email from Mervyn informs me he's got an interview at KaDeWe in ladies' accessories.

He also tells me that Jang-Mi and Woong have given up the course and returned to Korea. When she started drinking again, he put her on a plane and took her home. The admirable Milica has left to get private lessons, and is reported to have become practically fluent. He also proposes that we meet up with Karole some time. "Brunch at my place – apple martinis!" I reply that I can think of nothing nicer, but receive no further communication.

News arrives from Karole in the form of an emoji-rich text.

> "Yannis and I are 4 months pregnant [three big grins, three hearts for eyes, three champagne bottles, three party crackers, three cakes]. "So exciting. We are getting married in 5 weeks countdown. We just made the decision last week and it's been go go go ever since. 6 weeks to plan a wedding while pregnant is no joke. I just need to breathe [six faces with squiggles for mouths]. How are you guys doing???"

Roberto, having thrown his flat-warming party while I was rehearsing *Macbeth*, pops up to suggest we have a coffee together. Knowing him to be a man more in touch with a grand gesture than the granular detail, I set about the task of pinning him down to time and place.

...

What remains of a snowfall overnight has turned to ice, but, undeterred, I arrive punctually at Einstein's coffeeshop on busy Friedrichstraße. Waiting for Roberto, I open a book, though it's hard to concentrate. Groups of steaming tourists rest loudly between shopping bouts at the Christmas markets, and two young Americans at the next table compare notes on the artistic life with the vocal subtlety of a firing range manned by kids.

Eventually, Roberto shows up, panting through many layers of woolliness.

There are three Einstein cafés on Friedrichstraße, and, as he frees himself from his scarves, he informs me in German that he's been sitting in the wrong one for quarter of an hour. Struggling up Friedrichstraße against the crowds and the wind in sub-zero temperatures has cooled his natural warmth – or does he think it's my fault he can't read an email? He dumps his coat on mine and goes to order.

Ok, we seem to be speaking German. I rather hoped we'd do what we always do – begin in German and, within a sentence, slip into English, where we'd stay. This is going to be tricky. I'm a module and an exam behind, and rusty.

By the time he's thawed out and caffeined up, he strikes me as more serious than he was in class. He admits he's given up hope of ever being an archaeologist. "Maybe one day, as an amateur," he conjectures. "That's not so bad. That's quite good. I'd do the same stuff, just not get paid. But now I need a real job."

To which end, he's sat a test with the *BVG*, the company that runs Berlin's transport system, and if he passes, he'll undertake their three-year tram-driver's apprenticeship. They'll provide him a small wage, pay his rent and more or less guarantee a proper job at the end. Teasing him, I recall the time he told us about his dream. To jog his memory, I do an impression of him sitting back in his chair, imitating an F1-style driver, one-handedly slaloming round chicanes. But he doesn't remember the incident.

It's when he recounts the triumph that was his flat-warming party that the warm, chummy classmate I remember finally reappears in front of me. Gabbling with glee, he boasts that everyone from A-2-2 showed up to his flat – even Milica. Even the

Arab ladies! Of course there were drugs – Mira did MDMA! – but there was a special room for it, so no one was offended.

Gosh, I don't suppose even Karole could have finessed that.

He announces he has to make a move before I've had a chance to ask about Francesca, so, as he wraps himself back up in his scarves, he happily reports her good news: a promotion from dinner lady to teacher-assistant.

On the street, we agree to stay in touch, and part company with a hug. Wheeling into the tempest whipping up Friedrichstraße, he sets off one way, and with the wind behind me, I go the other. When I reach my bike, I look back to see if he's reached his. But he's already disappeared into the crowd.

Tim Luscombe is a writer, director and European. Born in London, he has worked and homed in many European countries and has now settled in Berlin, where he lives with his partner.

His plays and more recently this book celebrate Europe as they attempt to define European identity.

Other writing includes plays with gay and queer themes and several adaptations of nineteenth century English novels.

Before concentrating on writing, Tim worked as a director in the theatre. As well as being responsible for plenty of plays in the West End and on Broadway, he ran the London Gay Theatre Company in the 1990s.

For more information on Tim's work, please visit
www.timluscombe.com

If you enjoyed *Learning German (badly)* then check out other great books from **Claret Press**.

Claret Press publishes political fiction and creative non-fiction. While all our books have a political edge, we mean politics in the widest meaning of the word, from the esoteric to the commercial. We love stories that introduce readers to new ideas, unexplored places and pivotal events both here in the UK and across the globe.

Claret Press books inform, engage and entertain.

To know more about our books, like us on Facebook or subscribe to our website **www.claretpress.com**

Printed by BoD™in Norderstedt, Germany